To Erica
With best wishes
Enjoy the stories and
keep playing our great game.

"Alex. Aitchison has worked tirelessly to put tennis back on a big scale."
—Greg Hobbs, *Melbourne Sun News,* Australia, January 1972.
(Courtesy of the *Herald & Weekly Times* Pty. Ltd.)

"We are very sorry to lose Mr. Aitchison. He has been a conscientious and excellent officer for us. The Association will now advertise for two positions instead of a single management role."
—Ian Carson, President, The Lawn Tennis Association of
   Victoria, Melbourne, Australia, April 1972.

"Dear Alex.: You run a fine tournament. The qualifying event for the U.S. Open has turned into a mini-open and I know the problems connected with it are un-ending, but I would never know that from you. The event comes off so smoothly that perhaps you should consider running the U.S. Open. My sincerest thanks to you for the unbelievable job you do. I am deeply grateful for your efforts."
—William "Bill" Talbert, Tournament Director,
   1974 United States Open Tennis Championships

"The feeling is that there is a little magic weaved by Alex. Aitchison, who may be the master of all tournament mechanics."
—Murray Janoff, *Tennis Week,* March 1976
   (Courtesy of *Tennis Week* Magazine)

"Your tremendous organizational abilities and excellent rapport with players and tournament people alike resulted in a successful American Express Challengers Circuit."
—Warner J. Canto Jr., American Express Circuit, March 1977

In his announcement that Alex. Aitchison was resigning from the Eastern Tennis Association Junior Tennis Council Chairmanship, President Harry Marmion stated, "It will take two to fill his shoes. He will be sorely missed."
—*Tennis Week,* December 1980

"The philosophy that Alex. Aitchison follows in teaching the game of tennis is not necessarily to produce champions, but to teach youngsters to enjoy the game, and to develop their potential to the fullest, at the same time."
—John Parsons, *Tennis Today*, Great Britain, November 1980

"Dear Alex.: On behalf of my team, may I say how much I appreciated you being in Portland for our Davis Cup match. It was most reassuring to know that you were nearby and always willing to solve some of the little problems that come up in a match such as the semi-final."
—Neale A. Fraser, Australian Davis Cup Captain, October 1981

"Dear Alex.: Thanks so much for all that you do to make tennis better and our jobs so much easier; and many, many thanks for being so helpful to me."
—Alice Tym, Women's Tennis Coach, Yale University, February 1982

"Alex. Aitchison: Articulate, seasoned, tactful, diplomatic, a distinguished professional. It is a privilege to work with you."
—Robert Towers, Robert Towers Advertising, November 1982

Alex. Aitchison, Tournament Director, U.S.T.A. Olympic Tennis Trials.
"You did a marvelous job as tournament director and the fact that there were no visible problems is a tribute to your fine talents and work."
—Barbara S. Williams, Regional Vice-President, United States Tennis Association, June 1984

"Dear Alex., thank you so much for the courtesies you extended to me and my sons, Bill and Harry Gonzo, when we visited you last week. It was good of you to escort us about the premises and explain the different facets of the (national) tennis center to us. We

deeply appreciate everything you did to make our visit such a pleasant one. Sincerely, Bill."
—William H. Hudnut III, Mayor, City of Indianapolis, September 1985

"Dear Alex., I am writing to thank you very much indeed for arranging such excellent tickets for us and our Australian guests at the U.S. Open. It was very generous of you and I was delighted to have the opportunity to renew contact with John Newcombe and Rod Laver, whom I had not seen for some years. With personal regards and best wishes, Dick."
—Richard Woolcott, Permanent Representative of Australia to the United Nations, September 1985

"Alex. Aitchison has risen to become a big man in U.S. tennis and one of the most senior officials on the U.S. Tennis Association. The Port Washington Tennis Academy, where he is the director, is one of the most respected teaching facilities in the country and he is an influential voice in junior tennis."
—Richard Yallop, *Melbourne Age News,* Australia, 1985

"The United States Professional Tennis Association recognizes Alex. Aitchison for dedication toward self-improvement in tennis teaching and business and management skills, as shown by attending the 1987 High Tech Tennis U.S.P.T.A. National Convention."

"Dear Alex., I would like to express my deepest appreciation for your dedication and commitment as Chairman of the (national) Junior Tennis Council and as a member of the Olympic committee. Without your support and hard work, I truly could not have fulfilled my obligations and achieved some of my goals. Randy."
—J. Randolph Gregson, President and Chairman of the Board, United States Tennis Association, December 1986

"Alex. takes us back to some very interesting times in the tennis world with his fascinating stories about intriguing individuals who all contributed to the fabric of our tennis history. He takes us back before bringing us up to date and shares with us some of his own unique experiences he encountered along the way. Anyone who has an interest in this great sport, or was part of it, will enjoy this book. His sharp contemporary observations leave no doubt about informing and entertaining you. It is an honor to comment on a legend."

—Pete Summers, Host of TV's *Tennis Talk Show* and Host of the WLAD Radio *Pete Summers and the Morning Team Show*, December 2004

A Tennis Experience and All That . . .

A Tennis Experience and All That...

Alex. B. Aitchison

VANTAGE PRESS
New York

Excerpts from *15th Annual Eastern Tennis Hall of Fame Journal*, by Nancy Gill McShea, copyright © 2002, used by permission.
Excerpts from "Newtown Sports Hall of Fame 2001—Alex Aitchison," by Kim Harmon, copyright © 2001, courtesy of Kim Harmon and the *Newtown Bee*.
Excerpts from "Sports—Aitchison Heading to Hall," by Kim Harmon, copyright © 2002, courtesy of Kim Harmon and the *Newtown Bee*.
Excerpts from "Tennis Pro, 71, Being Honored for His Dedication to Volunteerism," by Chip Reid, copyright © 2002, courtesy of *Danbury News-Times*.

FIRST EDITION

All rights reserved, including the right of reproduction in whole or in part in any form.

Copyright © 2006 by Alex. B. Aitchison

Published by Vantage Press, Inc.
419 Park Ave. South, New York, NY 10016

Manufactured in the United States of America
ISBN: 0-533-15295-X

Library of Congress Catalog Card No.: 2005906455

0 9 8 7 6 5 4 3 2 1

To

My wife, Marjorie

My son, Perry

My son, Grant, and daughter in-law, Dawn
And their children, Julie and Michael

My son, Scott, and daughter in-law, Christin
And their children, Alec, Tyler, and Emily

Contents

Foreword   xiii
Acknowledgments   xv
A Message from the Author   xvii

1. Australia   1
2. Getting Started   3
3. A Brush with Death—Part One   6
4. Dunlop—The Start of a Sports Career   14
5. Allan Stone   24
6. Marjorie—Part One   26
7. Kooyong—Haunt of the Wild Fowl   31
8. Civil Defense   46
9. Richard Alonzo "Pancho" Gonzalez   49
10. Coming to America   51
11. The Port Washington Tennis Academy   54
12. John McEnroe   61
13. Irving V. Glick, M.D.: A Friend Indeed   65
14. The Eastern Tennis Association   70
15. The Rolex International Junior Tennis Championships   77
16. Andre Agassi   81
17. S.T.A.R.T.— Sports Technique and Reaction Training   84
18. The United States Tennis Association   87
19. In Quest of Excellence   115
20. The Chiquita Cup   124

21. People	129
22. Henry Christian Hopman	137
23. Volunteering	139
24. Remington International Family Tennis Championships	143
25. Memorable Occasions	150
26. A Brush with Death—Part Two	153
27. Tennis Consultants International, Inc.	159
28. Beaver Brook Tennis Club	163
29. Newtown Tennis Association	169
30. College Coaching	178
31. Marjorie—Part Two	184
32. Halls of Fame	187
33. Treasures	200
34. Closure	203
About the Author	205

Foreword

I first met Alex. Aitchison when I was a teenager in the early seventies. I had grown up close to the Port Washington Tennis Academy in New York, had known of its growing reputation for tennis excellence, and was delighted when my parents decided I could experience the place for myself.

Back then tennis was booming and all my idols were Aussies—Rod Laver, John Newcombe, Emerson and Hoad and Rosewall. They represented class and style, grace and sportsmanship. The Port Washington Tennis Academy was headed up by the great Harry Hopman, the Davis Cup coach who was so instrumental in bringing out the best in these players and bringing glory to Australia and the game itself. I wanted to learn how they played, how they trained, what they believed in. I wanted to be Australian, or at least be around them.

I got to know Mister Hopman and his Australian righthand man, Mister Aitchison. They were never called anything else by any of us kids. If you were serious about your tennis, and boy was I, you were serious about following protocol, obeying the rules, and respecting authority. Immediately I adored the place. It was alive with action, vitality, yearning. It was busy and bold and I tried hard to prove I belonged in such an environment. In a very short time everything else in my young life came second to tennis and my days at the Port Washington Tennis Academy. It became my world and the people who populated it became my best friends, my family. I spent every day of my life there, striving to be the kind of person an Aussie would like.

Alex. Aitchison (even all these years later I want to call him "Mister") helped to give me my wondrous childhood, a time that created my adult life in tennis. He's done this for so many people in so many places, in tennis and beyond the court as well. This book is a look back at how his life took shape, took hold in America, and took off into his remarkable journey in tennis. I'm so grateful that it all happened, and that I was one of the kids he took along for the ride.

—Mary Carillo

Acknowledgments

It would have been impossible for me to write this book if it had not been for the support that I received from my family and friends. I have also received so much encouragement from the tennis fraternity that it makes me proud to have belonged to such a high profile and prestigious group.

My everlasting gratitude to my wife Marjorie, for her patience and willingness to critique my work.

To my family, Perry, Grant and Dawn, and Scott and Christin for their belief in me, that I could achieve my goal.

The cover of this book is truly enhanced by two of my grandchildren, Alec and Tyler, whose faces will never be seen by the reader.

My sincere thanks to my friend Bob Nash whose personal time and photographic expertise made the cover possible, and for his great knowledge and advice on the world of books and computers, which he shared with me.

For making historic videos available for research, my friend, Tory Kiam of Remington Products.

Special gratitude to my close friends, who over the years found the time to write an unsolicited testimonial on my behalf. Warner Canto, Mary Carillo, Ian Carson, Neale Fraser, Randy Gregson, Greg Hobbs, Bill Hudnut, Murray Janoff, Billie Jean King, Harry Marmion, John Parsons, Pete Summers, Bill Talbert, Robert Towers, Alice Tym, Dennis Van der Meer, Barbara Williams, Dick Woolcott and Richard Yallop. Some of you have gone on to another world, but wherever each of you are, there or here, thank you with all of my heart.

To Anastasia Batzer whose literary expertise was shared with me in the early stages of my writings and allowed me to proceed with reasonable competence.

Many times I found myself floundering with my word processing and my good friend Colin Robertson was always there, day or night, to help this old man with his new toy. Thank you, Colin.

To my many friends who helped me with my research and to all of those wonderful people in chapter twenty-one. You are the ones who made this book possible. I will never forget you.

Finally, to my publisher Vantage Press, their editorial staff, their publicity and marketing departments, and all of the staff who strive for excellence and success on behalf of their authors.

A Message from the Author

My first thoughts about writing this book came in 1985.

I was in hospital for evaluation of pain in my neck and shoulders and numbness down my right side. The vehicular accident I was involved in, in 1984 (see chapter 26), accounted for this unwanted but necessary visit that looked very much like heading for the surgeon's table.

Lying on that sick bed, uncomfortable in every respect (why can't they make hospital beds comfortable?), wondering if and when the pain would go away, was unbearable, but what could I do?

One day, a nurse said to me, "Thinking about things that you have done, or want to do, might help you take your mind off the pain." I really was not convinced that that would help, but with the unknown certainty of pending surgery, I started to recall some of the things I had done in my life. No, it did not help a great deal.

Many mental pictures flashed through my mind but the reality of me being an author did not hit home at that time.

It was not until 1994 when I finally had the inevitable surgery on my neck, that I started to think again about putting some of my experiences on paper. I had often told stories to my friends in tennis and had always been encouraged to write about them. So, in 1999 I got serious, and made the decision to go ahead. I had no idea it would take so long.

Now, where was I to start? A lot of my material was not

documented, particularly from my Australian days, and I would have to rely heavily on my memory.

As there were so many happenings, my first step was to decide what stories would be appealing to a reader. I tested them out on friends, acquaintances and anyone else who would listen, mentally recording their reactions and responses, until I had a plan.

I know that there are many episodes told to eager ears that are not in this book, but those who have heard them have been able to share them with me firsthand, instead of having to read about them.

Memory or research may not have accurately recorded some of the events, but the vast majority of these words are of public record.

I hope you get as much pleasure reading about these experiences as I did writing about them.

A Tennis Experience and All That...

1
Australia

Australia, the land down under: a diverse land that boasts climates ranging from cool sea breezes in the South, crossing desolate arid deserts in the Center to the lush tropics in the North and along the Southeast coast the Alpine regions where the snowfields are bigger than the whole of Switzerland.

In the summer on a clear night you can lie prone on your back and watch the galaxies appear in the sky and wonder how it all can happen. First to appear is the "Evening Star" quickly followed by another star here, and before you can blink an eye, another one there, and soon the heavens are filled with the majesty of twinkling lights. The "Southern Cross" appears, the "Big Dipper," and the "Little Dipper", like two upside-down cooking pots, take their place alongside the "Milky Way" which stretches like a solid band of light for the full spectrum of your vision. On some occasions you can see the shooting stars going from one side of the sky to the other and your imagination runs wild as you envisage a tennis ball being hit backward and forward. Could it be that the angels play tennis? Soon the moon comes over the horizon and its brilliance dims the spectacular show that no fireworks display can match; but, if you miss it, it can be seen all over again tomorrow night.

Australia is the home of countless varieties of animals,

birds, fish and flora that are unique to that land, and is home to one of the most spectacular coral reefs in the world in the Great Barrier Reef, which has to be seen to be believed. This can be done by viewing the teeming marine life through glass bottom boats. It is a progressive land, able to hold its head high with counterparts around the world in the fields of agriculture, architecture (both old and new); art, culinary expertise, education, medicine, military power, science and sport, among other things. The people are friendly, outgoing and have a vernacular all of their own. Some of these sayings would be strange indeed to the visitor from another country. For instance; if you were being greeted, most likely it would be "G'Day Mate," or you could be invited to a "Barbie" (BBQ) where you might be asked to pass the "Dead Horse" (in Australia ketchup is called tomato sauce). In any case, you will find most Australians to be "Dinkum" (genuine/honest) people.

As opposed to the months that people in the northern hemisphere associate with the seasons, they are exactly opposite in the southern hemisphere where spring is September–November, summer is December–February, fall, March–May, and winter, June–August.

This is where I was born. This is where I grew up. This is where the first seeds of my tennis experiences were sown.

2
Getting Started

Tennis for me started in 1939 at the age of 8 when World War II broke out. For obvious reasons, with shortages of everything, it was not the best time to start on a new venture; however, I knew then that I wanted to be a tennis player but did not realize that it would be another four years before I got my real break to get involved in the game.

My brother, George, was a part-time tennis instructor at a local public court facility in the Melbourne suburb of Essendon, where we lived, and it was here that I learned to pick up balls and trash, to wind down the nets at the end of play for the day, sweep the courts and be a general helper. I loved to be there with him and the players who frequented the facility, and to feel that I belonged in this environment. My reward was to have George hit a few balls to me before we went home.

I know now, it was there that I learned the fundamentals of the game, even though at the time I could not fully understand what I was doing. It was to me a great time to be growing up in the game, and the popularity of the sport was evident. Wherever you looked, there seemed to be public tennis courts on every corner, much the same way that there are gasoline service stations occupying those same pieces of real estate today.

It was not until I went to Technical College, however,

that I really got involved in competition. Technical College and High School were equivalents in Australia in those days and the choice of which one you attended was based on what your academic desires and working future might be. But choices were limited then due to the concluding years of World War II. It was a difficult time to grow up; the economy was not healthy, jobs were difficult to get and luxury pastimes like tennis were limited because of the cost.

Perhaps the godsend for me and my tennis was that a good number of churches had tennis courts and a form of competition.

After graduating from Technical College and completing my tennis program there, "church" tennis was my next step in the "learning to play the game" phase. Here I was playing adult tennis and finding out what the game was all about and what it meant to win and lose gracefully.

There were no real Junior Tournaments in my growing up days except for State and National Championships and a few clubs that sponsored events for up-and-coming young players. Finances, or I should say, the lack thereof, precluded me from traveling to tournaments where I could gain valuable on court experience and the much needed competition that is so necessary to enhance one's ability in attaining greater heights.

Apart from my brother George, who had now moved to Sydney, some six hundred miles away, no one else in the family was really interested in tennis, so I fought the battle alone. My mother and stepfather moved to the country and I moved in with an aunt and whilst there, gained my independence and my driver's license which enabled me to travel.

By the time I had reached my 18th birthday I was playing local club tournaments held on weekends, and was satisfied that I was developing into a reasonable player. These events led to my participation in what was called the "pennant competition," also played on weekends, but in an Inter-club format. This competition catered for over 20,000 players representing approximately 4,500 teams and was divided into six levels of ability, the highest being at the "A" or "State" level. The remarkable thing about these numbers is that they were just representative of the Melbourne metropolitan area, Australia's second largest city.

Pennant tennis was the arena in which you progressed to the upper levels of the game and eventually into State and National competition. Here you might be noticed by the Davis Cup (men) or Federation Cup (women) selectors and be invited to some of their training sessions if they felt you had potential. Many young aspiring players would have their hopes dashed at this point in their careers, if they did not reach the pool of twenty or so from which the teams were selected. It was only the top six to twelve in the nation that got to travel and play in the important events under the auspices of the Lawn Tennis Association. Most National Championship draws were made up of visiting overseas players with the Australian participation percentage being small in comparison.

I was not disappointed and realizing the situation, was content to play in the "pennant" format. It is interesting to note that in 1966 I would eventually be responsible for running and maintaining this program, as well as playing in it, as the General Manager of the Lawn Tennis Association of Victoria.

In addition, a group of us at about the same level started our own singles competition, had a trophy made for the occasion, and played on a weekly basis. It was my honor to be the holder of that trophy on two occasions. This competition enhanced our overall goals and provided an extra challenge to each of us participating.

3
A Brush with Death—Part One

I cannot remember exactly how old I was, but I must have been about 7 or 8 when that first fearful episode took place. It was certainly before I got involved in tennis and could have resulted in me never playing the game. Our family had been visiting an aunt and uncle in a country area outside of Melbourne, and it was the morning of our return. We were driving into the railroad station to catch the once-only-each-day train back to Melbourne. I can recall that my uncle was driving, my stepfather was in the front passenger seat and I was in the back.

My mother was staying in the town with another relative, and we were to pick her up on the way.

The road was a typical country dirt road and I have no concept of what happened to cause our accident. For whatever reason, we had struck the roadside railing of an under-road culvert, taking down all four posts with their three rows of railings, careened off the bank, struck a tree which snapped off, propelling the car into the air. It landed upside down resting on the roof. My only memory of the accident is crawling out through the back door and seeing the gasoline pouring from the tank. My stepfather and uncle were also able to crawl out from the wreckage and thankfully no one was seriously hurt. My stepfather had a cut eyebrow and we all had minor lacerations and bruises along with soreness for a week or two.

Fortunately, a farmer at a nearby farm had heard the noise of the crash and immediately came to our aid. We were taken to his home and the necessary telephone calls were made to police and doctors and my mother. It goes without saying that we missed the train but we were happy that we were all in one piece. Being as young as I was, I gave little thought at the time as to how close this was to a fatality.

At age 20 I was very much into tennis and wanted to play tournaments and competitions, but these cost money that I did not have. A friend who was a limousine driver suggested that I might like to try chauffeuring as the compensation was excellent, and the hours flexible enough to fit in with my tennis program. He arranged an interview for me, which was successful, and I got started on a new career. Driving was a passion with me and I loved the feeling of being in control of those big black shining limousines and the pride that came with presenting an immaculate method of transportation to my passengers. I might add that I put my age up by two years to get this prestigious position. Never once did I feel I should doubt the integrity of the people I would have in my vehicle for after all this was a limousine. However, this was not to be.

I had elected to work the night shift from 6 P.M. to 6 A.M. as this was the lucrative time with people going out to dinner and the theatre, and returning home. More often than not, it was usual to pick up the same people at the conclusion of their evening out, that you had driven earlier. While fares were standardized, gratuities were free flowing and would often exceed the cost of the fare if the customer had had a good time. In spite of all the good times, I had three instances as a limousine driver that helped me make the decision to look for some other means of financial support for my tennis and living needs.

The first was, I had been sent to an address in an inner suburb of Melbourne at about 9 P.M. to pick up a client named "Bill" and take him to "other destinations." I rang his doorbell and he answered gruffly through the door; "Wait in the car, I will be there in a minute." I got into my car and started my meter to measure the waiting time and waited.

About 15 minutes later, this man whose appearance matched his voice, came out carrying a duffle bag and got into the backseat. His simple statement was, "Drive." When I asked him where to, again it was, "Just drive"—so I drove. Every once in a while he would direct me up this street and down that street, all of which to me seemed rather strange and futile. I was about to ask him if there was a final destination plan when I noticed a slight movement alongside of my head on the back of the front seat. I instinctively turned my head and to my amazement it was the barrel of a sawed-off shotgun. This was the first time I had ever encountered a situation like this and I froze. I stopped the car and said, "What is going on?" He replied, "I told you to drive, now drive; I'm looking for the bastard who is fooling around with my wife and when I find him he's dead meat."

Amid my fear I had no idea how I was going to get out of this, so I drove, never taking my eyes off the road but clearly seeing the barrel of that gun at all times. Soon after, "Bill" directed me to stop alongside a vacant building lot. Across the other side was a group of small tenement houses. He got out of the car with his duffle bag and said to me, "Stay put and don't have any idea of leaving; I'm gonna see if he is over there."

I watched him walk across the lot and start to go around the back of one of the houses and in the street lights I could see him undoing the bag as he disappeared. For about half a minute I was frozen, remembering his warning, but then I decided to make a break for it. I took off like I was in the Grand Prix of car racing and headed for home and locked the doors. I was so fearful of him catching up with me that I did not go to work for a week. Even then, it was about two months before I stopped looking over my shoulder.

A report was filed with the police giving them all of the details but their investigation failed to come up with anything that would allow them to prosecute. "Bill" had disappeared, no one had been murdered, so nothing further came of the incident.

The second occasion was another experience with a gunman. It was one o'clock in the morning and I was to pick up a Mr. Peters and take him to Frankston, wait and return.

The pickup was at a hotel in the inner-city part of Melbourne. From a monetary point of view this was a good paying fare as Frankston was on the outer suburban limits and the job would take two hours or more, depending on the waiting time. I picked up Mr. Peters who was a middle-aged, well-dressed man carrying a small overnight bag. The trip was pleasant with agreeable conversation and took about an hour. As we drove into the outskirts of the city he said, "I will give you directions," and shortly after, as we approached a small group of shops, he pointed out a TV and Electrical shop on the opposite side of the road. He said, "Turn the car around and park in front of that store and leave the motor running." Immediately I knew there was something amiss—who would be visiting an appliance store at this time of the morning, unless you were the owner, but to leave the motor running, no, this was all wrong. I got my answer straightaway when I felt something cold on the back of my neck and Mr. Peters said, "This is a gun and I'm not afraid to use it."

As we pulled up in front of the store he told me to, "Sit still and be ready to move quickly when I tell you, I'll be watching you." He got out of the car, went to the door of the store, and gained entry with tools from the bag he was carrying. Once again I was faced with the decision of, do I stay or run? There was no doubt in my mind now that this was a robbery and my passenger had unwittingly done me a favor by telling me to leave the motor running. I sneaked a look sideways and could not see him through the store window so assumed he could not see me. Slowly I eased myself down into the seat so that I could just see the road ahead, slipped the car into gear (there were no automatic drive vehicles in Australia then), and drove out of there as if all the demons out of hell were after me. It was interesting to note that not one other vehicle went by during the ten minutes or so that I was there. Again, a police report was filed but I never heard of a robbery in Frankston on that date. I assumed that the would-be thief took off soon after me, to avoid capture.

Needless to say I did not collect any fare money from either of my two criminal passengers.

My third episode was a vehicular one. I had taken passengers to a destination in the southern suburbs of the city and was returning to my base in the northern area at about 10 o'clock in the evening. It had been raining, the roads were wet, vision was poor, and generally it was not a pleasant time to be driving. I was traveling on a secondary road and approaching an intersection with the green light in my favor. As I entered the intersection I saw a car entering on my left at high speed against the red light. To avoid impact was impossible. In a failed desperate attempt to miss it I swerved, but not before hitting the trunk area and spinning this vehicle around like a top. I had a recollection of a body being part way out of the car before my limo flipped over landing upside down on its roof. Remarkably I was not hurt, except for some bumps, which became bruises eventually, and was able to crawl out from the wreckage.

I went over to the other car and a young lady was getting out from the passenger side. She confirmed that her door had opened due to the impact and that she had struggled furiously to stay inside the vehicle. Her head, however, had made contact with the ground and she had the lacerations to prove it. (Seat belts were not yet in vogue.) Her boyfriend was unhurt but stunned and shaken, as we all were, and admitted to me that it was all his fault as he was not concentrating on his driving. Because of a potentially serious head injury to the young lady, we needed help fast I went to my car to see if the two-way radio was still working, and fortunately it was. I called my home base, told them what had happened and requested that they call the police, the ambulance, send a tow truck, and another car to get me home. They all arrived in short time and everyone was checked out by the medical team, the vehicles cleared from the road, and we were taken to the police station to file reports. The other driver admitted negligence with no fault to me; the young lady refused medical treatment, and to maintain my confidence, I drove our other car back to base. Two months later, the other driver and his girl friend tried to bring a law suit against me, but their claim of negligence and cause of injury was dismissed due to the on-scene evidence and police reports.

Much later in my life, at the age of 35, I was diagnosed with diabetes during a necessary medical checkup when I changed my working career from Dunlop to the Lawn Tennis Association of Victoria.

Although I was still active in tennis and squash, I was not the fine-tuned athlete anymore, which was necessary for playing high level competition. I had become an administrator, gained weight, and was smoking seventy cigarettes a day. It was a standing joke that if you wanted to see Aitchison, after you opened his office door you had to swim through the smoke. The weight, heavy smoking and stress of the job were all natural ingredients for the disease that I was diagnosed with in 1966. Unfortunately the lack of knowledge about diabetes in those days did not stimulate serious interest and it was not until July of 1969 that I got my shock treatment.

Typically my work time at the Lawn Tennis Association averaged between 70 and 90 hours per week, and I had come home one evening after an exceptionally exhausting 12–14 hour day, and was extremely hungry. I virtually "wolfed" down the meal that my wife had prepared for me and immediately had severe indigestion. I took the normal antacids to combat my discomfort but they did not work; there was no alternative, I simply had to go to bed. I quickly got undressed and climbed into bed hoping that exhaustion would overcome discomfort, and that I would fall asleep. This was not to be. As soon as I lay down I knew something was radically wrong; I could not breathe and I felt I was losing consciousness. I tried to raise my hands to bang on the wall to get my wife's attention, but could not raise them.

We owned an "L" shaped house in those days and our bedroom suite was at the opposite end to the living room, where I had left my wife. Fortunately for me, she thought I looked pretty awful when I went to bed, and came to see if I was alright. There is little remembrance of what happened after that, except that I do recall our family doctor, the great four-mile Olympic runner John Bartram, making the house call and stabbing me with the biggest needle I had ever seen, then and to this day. His quick action of quieting me down and releasing the panic, saved me from a fatal heart attack.

Some of the characteristics of my former fitness days

had helped in allowing a natural by-pass to take place. It took some three months of recuperation before I was allowed back to work, and a most definite life-style change. No more smoking; I quit cold turkey, and have not wanted one since; a change in dietary habits, which really did not get serious until we moved to the United States in 1972. There was just not enough knowledge about the complications of diabetes in the '60s, and I had not come to terms with my problem. If I had, perhaps this episode could have been avoided.

I am pleased to say now, some 35 plus years later, that good control over my diet, diligently supervised by my wife, coupled with a daily exercise program, allows me to live an almost normal life.

4
Dunlop—The Start of a Sports Career

In October of 1951 I had the good fortune to join the staff of Dunlop Rubber Australia Limited, at the Melbourne head office. I was placed in their footwear division controlling and monitoring the Company's vast variety of sporting footwear.

Just before Christmas of that same year, the sports promotion manager of the sporting goods division had learned that I played tennis and asked me if I would like to represent the company at a Christmas country tournament. I accepted eagerly.

At that time country tennis tournaments were a part of the ladder system for the game where players could hone their skills on surfaces such as asphalt, clay, concrete, plain old dirt that had been leveled by a piece of farm machinery, grass, and even "ant bed" material.

Ant bed material is the underground tunnel refuse of the huge two-inch-long bush ants as they built their kingdoms far below the surface of the earth. They would bring this finely excavated soil to the surface, where they would fashion perfectly cone-shaped towers, some of which might stand six or seven feet high. This material, although rare for tennis courts, was one of the most pleasant surfaces to play on.

Most of the country tournaments were played on holiday weekends such as Christmas, New Year's, Australia Day, Labor Day and Easter, and their numbers were around fifty or so for the season, giving players a wide variety to choose from. They were strongly supported by the sporting goods manufacturers as a promotional activity and many of the "free list" players (those who received equipment in return for representation), from the three major companies—Dunlop, Slazenger and Spalding—went to these events in return for the tennis ball adoption of the tournament or the inter-club ball usage of the Associations who ran them.

I had some of the most pleasant experiences in my tennis life at these events, including proposing to my wife over a bottle of milk, at the end of a hard day's play. On almost every occasion it was a group of friends who got together as a team to go to a particular tournament, and our motto was "play hard, play your best tennis, and have a good time." I cannot remember a single tournament where the local organizers failed to provide us city slickers with bounteous food supplies and entertainment in the evenings, either in their homes or the local halls. Usually the bigger events would have players from the "big three" and this made for interesting and challenging competition to see who could take home the most titles and trophies.

At one particular event I had been seeded fairly high and was expected to be in at least the last four of the men's singles championship. Well, expectation and reality often do not work together. I played so poorly (or was it that I got thrashed by a better player?) that I was ousted in the second round. I have to admit that in those days I was a feisty player and did not always keep my emotions under control. The match was played on day two late in the afternoon and finished just about the time when the host club was preparing for a player Barbie (BBQ) and welcome party. At the conclusion of the match I recall that I went straight to the fires, which were already glowing hot, and placed both my rackets on as additional fuel. Rackets were of the wood variety then.

No words were spoken. Just amazement. The lesson: learn to lose gracefully.

Also, much to my shame, I had not been a good representative for my company.

Another tournament had me entered in six events to be played over three days. On the final day I was still in those six events and I can remember vividly playing one hundred and sixty-six games of tennis in sixteen hours, to close out that marathon. The day was so packed full of having to be on the court, that no time could be allocated to taking time off for food. Snacks, lunch and dinner were had as we changed ends. As luck would have it, we ran out of daylight and had to move to another club nearby that had lighted courts. This gave me a much needed break and a chance to have some proper nutrition and to catch my breath.

Time went by in a blur and finally we reached the last event; the mixed doubles final. The clock read just after 1 A.M. My partner, who was a local girl, and I had to play two others from our team that had come from Melbourne.

The referee of the tournament, a dairy farmer, was showing concern that he might have to go straight to milking his cows if this match went to three sets. As his milking time was usually around 5 A.M. he asked if we would consider playing a short match. He suggested a seven or nine game pro-set which was fine with my partner and me, but our opponents strongly argued for the regular best of three sets. As I was the driver responsible for getting our team back to Melbourne, including our opponents, who of course could sleep during the four hour return trip, and the fact that I had had such a grueling day, I wanted the short match.

We argued for some time and finally the referee said he would make the decision as we could not agree. His decision, best of three games. Even I was stunned, I had never heard of a championship final that short. He was correct in his decision however, as we could not resolve the problem and his was the final word.

To win the toss and the right to serve was important as one team would only get to serve once. We lost the toss and the first game. I elected to serve for our team and we leveled the score at 1–1. Now the challenge was to break our opposition and clinch the match. We were facing our female opponent who had a strong serve and was not going to go down easily. This game was one of the toughest I have ever played, but finally, after four deuces, we got the advantage and won the title.

We left the tournament site at around 2:30 A.M. and four plus hours later, with the sun shining through the back window of my car, I drove into my driveway and a bed that had been beckoning to me for hours.

Because of my tennis expertise, I was soon transferred to the Sports Goods Division where I became a metropolitan sales representative and after a short time graduated to Class "A," Provincial City and Major City accounts. Eventually I was moved up to the position of Sports Promotion Manager which I held until May of 1966. The prime specification of the job was to promote sales of the company's products through dealer and consumer avenues. This meant control over and use of company players in tournaments, clinics, exhibitions and any other facet that would enhance the company's image. All sports were under my control including badminton, cricket, football, golf, lawn bowls, squash, table tennis and tennis.

It was my pleasure to work and play with many of the

top players in the world in their respective sports, each one giving a great experience, and at the same time giving me an opportunity to learn from these great champions. I can attest to the fact that my ability to be an "all-rounder" was enhanced by being in contact with world class sports people such as Colin McDonald, cricket; Arnold Palmer, golf; Alec Eames, lawn bowls; Hashim and Roshan Khan, squash; Karol and Susie Javor, table tennis; and Rod Laver, tennis, to name a few. Of course, tennis being my first sporting love, provided me with unlimited opportunity for contact with the great champions of that game.

From World War II to the time I started working and playing for Dunlop, Australia seemed to produce tennis greats at will and most of them would cross my future path, predominately in the form of tournament activity. Names such as Alexander, Anderson, Bowery, Bromwich, Brown, Case, Cooper, Crawford, Crealy, Davidson, Dent, Dibley, Emerson, Fraser, Giltinan, Hartwig, Hoad, Laver, Long, MacNamee, Masters, McGrath, McGregor, McNamara, Newcombe, Pails, Roche, Rose, Rosewall, Ruffels, Sedgman, Stolle, Stone, Quist, Court-Smith, Dalton, Goolagong, Krantzke, Tegart and Turner competing against International greats Ashe, Connors, Gerulaitis, Graebner, Gonzalez, Kramer, Krishnan, Lutz, McKinley, Metreveli, Mulloy, Nastase, Osuna, Palafox, Parker, Perry, Pietrangeli, Ralston, Riggs, Santana, Schroeder, Segura, Seixas, Smith, Talbert, Trabert, Bueno, King, Moran, Moratsova, Navratilova, Richey and Wade, provided fuel for my fire for life, and these memories and experiences with them, are still burning brightly.

The job was not all fun, games and glory. Many hours were spent creating and administering methods of selling, preparing and setting up agendas for sales conferences, compiling and editing material for publication in magazines and journals, planning budgets and controlling their expenditures, carrying out promotional programs for schools through the education departments, conducting clinics and exhibitions for clubs and associations and representing the company in all levels of society.

One of these programs was planned for the Snowy River Tennis Association buried deep in the Snowy Mountains area some three hundred miles northeast of Melbourne. It was to take the form of a tennis clinic. There were six of us on our team and we left Melbourne by car at about 5 P.M. on a Friday night. Friday night travel is the same whichever country you are in; everyone trying to get out of the city for that nice weekend, creating those mind-boggling traffic jams.

We arrived at our destination hotel at about 1 A.M. on Saturday morning to find everything completely in the dark. Where was our welcoming committee? Our flashlight spotted a note on the door which read; "Welcome, door is unlocked, sandwiches and drinks are in the kitchen down the hall." These niceties were certainly well received after our long trip and we made short order of what was there. Also on the table were our room numbers and direction to the courts with the starting time of the clinic. Being that that was 10 A.M., we got to bed for a well deserved rest.

After being awakened and given a magnificent country breakfast, we headed for the courts. Arriving at our designated hour we were astounded that there was not a soul to be seen. About five minutes later, a man arrived on a bicycle and introduced himself as the President, after which he opened a small shack that also served as the clubhouse and a place to store nets, balls, brooms, etc. With much ado, he came out with a big bell (in country areas called a cow bell), and started swinging this thing like there was no tomorrow.

Backward and forward it went and the noise reverberated throughout the mountains until it seemed like one continuous piercing wail. It had the effect that was intended. The signal had been sent. Kids came from everywhere. They came on bicycles, with parents in cars; on horseback; out of the woods; and one even came by canoe down the river that ran by the courts. By ten-thirty everyone had arrived, all sixty of them. We had a dilemma! What do you do with sixty eager tennis children on four tennis courts?

With quick consultation our team came up with the answer. One of our group was a physical education teacher and right alongside of the tennis courts was a football field.

These future players were about to be introduced to the necessity of fitness training in order to be an athlete. My phys-ed teacher and one other instructor would take all but sixteen students to the football field and run them through fitness drills and shadow play.

Our on-court players would rotate from court to court in groups of four and we would use the football field as a fifth station. Every ten minutes a rotation would take place until everyone had rotated through the system, and we would repeat the procedure until all students had experienced every part of our program. Play was added in the latter part of the day. We repeated the format on Sunday and everyone seemed to have a good experience.

The hospitality of the tennis association and the Country Women's Association who provided the food and refreshments was outstanding and much appreciated by us who had put in two eight hour days on the court. Saturday evening had also been a huge success when we had an informal adult question and answer night.

Even though we were tired on the long six hour trip home, our spirits were high with the feeling that we had achieved our goal; that being, introducing many young people to the game. The reward for our efforts was a promise from the Tennis Association that they would use the Dunlop tennis ball in all of their matches and tournaments.

Another interesting scenario took place when this time we visited a larger town. Our team again had six players but this time we had eight courts at our disposal. Over sixty children had signed up for this one-day event, but there was no other field to filter the students into the instruction process. It meant that we would take eight players on each of four courts and our two remaining team members would take the balance on the other four to do fitness drills, shadow drills and play games. As it happened, the court structure was two banks of four and we were able to rotate groups with little or no inconvenience.

I was one of the single court instructors and placed my eight players so that I was hitting to four and had the other four behind me picking up balls and returning them to a box at my feet. Ball baskets were unheard of in those days.

The change from end to end was frequent so as to avoid boredom and maintain interest. On the very first change-over I was in trouble. I had hardly delivered the first balls to my new group when I was hit in the back by one of the ball retrievers. I turned around and said, "Please don't hit the balls back to me, pick them up on your racket and bring them to the box." I resumed my instruction only to receive another ball in the back and again I requested the balls be carried back to the box. I made another change of players and everything went smoothly.

Would you believe, when I rotated the groups again, it started all over. First a ball in the back of the leg, another got me in the neck, a third hit me in the thigh and I GOT MAD. I turned around and said, "If I catch the one who is doing this he is in trouble."

It was obvious there was a "smart" character in the group and I was determined to see who it was. A couple more balls went flying by and on impulse I turned around and caught the culprit in the act. He was a small boy with a cheeky face and I am sure he felt that he had gotten away with his mischief. I immediately walked back to him and said, "You have finished for the day and to make sure you don't annoy anyone else, I am going to hang you up on the fence." At most country tennis clubs, there is a hook or a nail on the fence here and there and right behind this kid was a hook just made for him. I picked him up and hung him on the hook by his shirt collar. Did it rip? Yes, it sure did, but he was hanging there much to the amusement of his friends and now crying because of what this big bully of a tennis instructor had done. I cannot say I was proud of my actions because in these situations I was usually a fairly placid character, but this kid really got to me.

The story does not end there as I was then confronted by an irate mother who could not believe that anyone would do this to her son. I agreed that my action was drastic but said it never would have happened if he had some respect for his elders. I asked her to take him home and promised that I would make amends. On my return to Melbourne I sent him three new shirts, some tennis balls and wrist bands. I never saw or heard from either of them again and just hoped that a lesson was learned.

Of course, I was afraid that the club would never use the Dunlop ball again because of my action, but this was not the case. The club officials had also had trouble with him on occasions, but no one was prepared to do anything. I was their scapegoat sent from heaven. Perhaps if they had taken some action with this young man in the early days of his bad behavior, this incident might never have happened and he would have been a nicer kid. In spite of the unpleasantness, they adopted our ball for all of their play.

There are hundreds of stories like this to tell another time, but these two are examples of the experiences that confront the promoter and at the same time, show the desire that Australian country clubs had in my time, in fostering the game of tennis to the young by providing a healthy recreation.

No other sporting activity provides the lifetime physical benefits to the body that tennis does. I have seen three-year-old tiny tots starting out, ninety-year-olds still hustling in their twilight days, and every age in between, all strutting their stuff and enjoying this wonderful game at their own level.

It truly can be said that TENNIS IS THE GAME FOR A LIFETIME.

5

Allan Stone

During my early promotional days at Dunlop Sports, one of my duties was to manage the "free list player" program. This was a group of players who received equipment in return for their representation at tournaments and exhibition play. They played an important role in enhancing the exposure of company products and motivating sales through various marketing programs.

One such tennis player was Allan Stone, an up-and-coming player who in the '60s had started to show talent that eventually would blossom into the world class arena.

My story goes back to that era when Allan was playing in the Australian Hardcourt Championships one year and trying desperately to break through into the upper ranks.

I had arrived to view his match after it had commenced and was standing behind the bleachers, out of sight, as I did not want him to have the pressure of me watching. He was an excellent player and seemed to have his match under control, when he missed an easy volley. You know, one of those that you just let the ball hit the strings and it goes nowhere. Not being classified as a mild mannered person, he smashed the racket on the ground and broke it. I quickly stepped back so that there was no chance of him seeing me as he selected another racket to continue his match.

The next morning, I received a phone call from him asking if he could come in for more rackets. I said, "Of course, how many do you need?" He replied, "Four would be good, would you have them strung for me?" As we kept special players' rackets in inventory (we made them to player specifications then), I was able to give him a pickup date and at the same time I said to him, "Allan, bring five dollars each for them when you come." There was silence on the other end for awhile but eventually he said, "Did you say I had to pay for them?"

"Yes," was my reply. "You have just become the first free list player to learn that if you break a racket in anger, you are going to pay for the replacement." I told him that I had seen his loss of control during the championships and he agreed that my decision was fair.

I did not lose him as one of my players and to his credit, he went on to represent Australia in Davis Cup competitions in 1970, 1976, 1978 and 1979.

6

Marjorie—Part One

Marjorie was the girlfriend of one of my group with whom I played tennis on a regular basis. She was a good looking girl and a proficient player in her own right, who came to watch her friend Colin and I play, as well as our other members. Somehow or other though, I never appreciated her good looks because it seemed to me that she was always talking to him through the fence about getting theatre tickets or some other chore that he was supposed to carry out. This annoyed me considerably and even though I would insist to Colin that she leave because it was upsetting my concentration and game, he never exerted himself to have her do that. Understandable, I guess, if it was helping him to win; this was his secret weapon.

Over time, we really developed a great dislike for each other and on my part, almost a hate relationship. On reflection, this was unfair, as she had never done anything to me to promote this feeling. Anyhow, life went on and we had nothing to do with each other for years. In fact, my only contact with her or her family was that I went to the same school as her brother John, who also played in our group.

One of the tennis competitions that I played in and liked the most was a mixed doubles inter-club program that was played on a Wednesday night starting at 8 P.M. Matches were played outdoors, often in misty rain or fog and consisted of men's doubles, women's doubles and mixed doubles. Sometimes the fog was so heavy that if you lobbed the ball above the lights, it was lost until it came back down under the sight line often disorientating your opponents. We used this as a tactic many times to regain position on the court after being pushed wide by an angle shot. Here is a lesson on the value of the lob when you need to recover and every split second counts.

In the early winter of 1957 our team, of which I was the captain, was doing well and we were headed for the finals. It was important to finish as high as possible in the final four, particularly at the number one position, because of the complicated formula used to play the final matches. The first two matches were between 1 versus 3 and 2 versus 4 then, using an example, it went like this. No. 1 team defeats No. 3 team and goes straight into the Grand Final. No. 2 team defeats No. 4 team and goes into a final berth. No. 3 and 4 teams play off with the winner to go into the final berth. No. 3 team defeats No. 4 team and plays No. 2 team in the final. No. 2 team defeats No. 3 team in the final and advances to the Grand Final to meet No. 1 team. No. 1 and No. 2 teams play off for the championship.

All of these matches took place over a four week period and it was easy to see how important it was to finish on top of the four.

We had reached the last home and away match and were set to go. The competition had been so close and intense throughout the season, being of the standard where some former and some hopeful Davis Cup players participated. The verdict as to which team would finish on top would be decided that night. The matches to be played were one men's doubles, one women's doubles and two mixed doubles with four players on each team. Each individual contest was to be a nine-game advantage pro set. This meant that if the score was eight games all, play continued until one team won by a margin of two games. The championship was decided by scoring individual matches first, sets won second, and games won third. In the event of a tie score, the Championship Team would be decided by cumulative scores and ladder standings over the season.

DISASTER struck at three-thirty on the afternoon of our big game. One of the ladies on our team was an airline attendant and had flown to Brisbane, some thousand miles or so to the north that morning and was due to return the same day and be ready for the match. Some minor thing with the aircraft had grounded them and she could not return in time to play.

I panicked. Substitutes had to be registered players and there were very few around at this late stage in the season. Out came the little black book and the phone began to buzz. By five-thirty I had exhausted my short list without success. What could I do? I was desperate, but there was one last chance to avoid defeat. Marjorie. Questions arose in my mind. Given our relationship, would I have the gall to ask her to play? Was she registered? Was she available to play? Would she play for someone like me who had shown so much disregard for her feelings?

Well, with time running out, I plucked up courage and made the call. It went something like this: "Hello Marjorie, this is Alex Aitchison and I have a problem that you might be able to help me with."

She responded, "What is the problem?"

I told her, "One of the players on our team match tonight is stuck in Brisbane and cannot get back and I desperately need a substitute to take her place. We are contending for the top position and do not want to default. Would you be willing to play for us? I know we have not been on the best of terms but the team and I would really appreciate it if you could help us out."

After brief silence, she replied, "Yes—I will play for you so that the team will not be disappointed." To my question about being a registered player, her answer was, "Yes, I am registered and cleared to play."

We were out of a deep hole, I could breathe again. I agreed to pick her up at her home at the appropriate time and thanked her again for helping us out. We drove to the club where the match was being played and I introduced her to the other members of the team. All was well.

Match time came around and the men were to play first. The tension in the air was electric due to the importance of the position that the winning team would have for the finals play. My partner and I lost a close 9–7 set, then Marjorie and her partner, who had not played together before, turned on the heat with some magnificent tennis to win 9–6.

As it was my partner who was stranded in Brisbane, Marjorie and I teamed up for the first mixed and unfortunately we lost another cliff-hanger 9–7.

Now we were faced with the final set which we just needed to win because the ladies with their 9–6 result had given us that one game advantage. Our team struggled from the moment they walked on the court. Usually a solid combination, nothing was going right.

Soon they were down 7–2 and I made the comment to Marjorie that the match was all over and that we would have to be satisfied with the number two spot. Much to my amazement she commented, "I think they will win."

I said, "How can you speculate like that when you don't even know their capabilities?"

She insisted that they would win and my sarcastic response was, "Look, I'm so sure they cannot win that I will take you out to dinner and a show if they do, and I don't particularly want to take you out."

What a jerk I was! Here was a girl who had just gotten us out of real trouble and I was treating her like a second-class citizen. Her silence told me of the hurt. . . . Our team fought back in magnificent style to take the set 9–7, giving us the match and the top position for the finals playoff. We won the championship that year beating the same team again in the Grand Final. Although Marjorie did not participate in that Grand Final match, she played a significant role in making it possible for us to achieve our goal.

For a reason I will never understand—or for that matter ever know—Marjorie agreed to take me up on my belligerent offer and have dinner with me. Strangely enough, we both enjoyed our evening and over a short time, our attitudes changed toward each other and we went out again. Then we started playing mixed doubles together, going to tournaments, joined the same clubs, developed common interests and on April 4th 1959, I made the best decision of my life; I married Marjorie.

It can be said that I lost a bet but won a wife.

7

Kooyong—Haunt of the Wild Fowl

In January of 1966 I was away on an extended four-to-six week promotion and sales trip to major accounts of Dunlop that were in the provincial cities and main towns in the country areas. On my return, I was calling on one of the major metropolitan "A" accounts, the Lawn Tennis Association of Victoria, which was the governing body of the second largest tennis state in Australia. The Association facility housed a club membership of around four thousand, maintained a thirteen thousand seat stadium, thirty-four grass courts, fourteen hard courts, squash courts, pro shop, a licensed restaurant, two liquor bars, member lounges and fully equipped locker rooms. In addition, in Victoria it administered the game with all of its complexities and ran major tennis events including Davis Cup, National and State Championships, Country and Metropolitan Championships and the largest Inter-club competition that one would ever wish to see.

In my discussions with the manager, he asked me why I had not applied for the position of assistant manager of the association; in his opinion it would be ideal for me and as we had a good relationship, we could work well together. The fact that the position was available was a surprise to me, and must have been advertised while I was away on my trip. In short, he said that he could get my application included and an interview arranged if I was interested. I filled out the necessary papers, eventually had my interview, successfully got the appointment, and started my duties in May of 1966.

It was not going to be long before there would be a major change in my assistant managerial duties. Australia was to play India in a Davis Cup challenge round at Kooyong in December of that year and preparations were already well under way and coming to a head. By way of explanation, in those days the Challenge Round was arrived at by all of the competing nations (except the defending nation), playing off to provide a challenger to compete against the champion from the previous year, for the Davis Cup title. I was heavily involved in the organization of the event and long hours were being put in by both the manager and myself. Two days before the tie was to commence the manager could not be found anywhere. He had not arrived at work and questions were being asked about the event, that only he could answer.

I called his home with no response (no answering machines then) and tried every conceivable place that he might be, without success. No one had seen him. I struggled through the day doing what I could to solve the last minute problems of a match with such magnitude and hoped that tomorrow would bring better results. The next day, the eve before this great event, our manager had still not come to work or called our office. We continued to try and make contact, calling his home and all those places he may have been, but to no avail.

The manager had disappeared.

The enormity of the situation suddenly became very real. The President of the Association, Australia's legendary Davis Cup captain, Harry Hopman, directed me to assume the role of manager and ordered me to "Get us through this thing." There was no time to feel inadequate about what had to be done and with the combined efforts of the tournament committee, the administrative staff and the grounds crew, the three day event went off without a hitch. The sellout crowd of thirteen thousand who attended each day were treated to outstanding tennis and perfect weather.

Australia retained the Davis Cup that year, defeating India four rubbers to one.

What an experience it was for me to be presenting such an event on the world stage of tennis so early in my administrative career. All through the weekend I had the feeling that the manager would show up, but he did not—ever.

A few months later, the Association, under its by-laws had to advertise to fill the managerial position and some fifty-seven applications were received by the search committee. I was advised to remain cool and continue with my duties until all applicants had been interviewed. It was a harrowing experience waiting for the process to be completed but in due course I was successful and continued on, not as acting manager, but as Chief Executive Officer of the Association and General Manager of Club Activities. The process of hiring an assistant commenced immediately.

The Association was a complex organization owning the land on which the facilities stood and functioned with a seventy-nine man council. This council was comprised of representatives from the executive officers, the membership, delegates from metropolitan clubs and associations, country and metropolitan regions and the umpires association. Their task was to administer the game in the State of Victoria. To achieve this there were thirteen working committees and each of them had at least three sub-committees, all of whose meetings I was required to attend.

My duties, which often took me ninety hours some weeks, were demanding to say the least. First and foremost was to administer all of the affairs of the Association and manage the complex. This would include being the chief negotiator with all parties interested in the promotion of the game such as the Sports Promotion and Tennis Promotion Councils, sponsors, etc., etc. This led to representation at all levels of society, making press, radio and television releases, appearances at functions, opening new clubs and courts and generally promoting association policy, objectives and activities. I was responsible for the coordination of the day-by-day operation of the working committees and their "subs" who governed the rules and conditions of play for the approximately three hundred thousand players in the State. My days were filled with the compilation of reports, budgets, minutes, magazines, etc., arranging training and coaching programs, setting up the classes and working with our professional staff on the development of our top juniors and the management of our office staff.

The most glamorous of regular activities was the conduct of the Australian championships (later the Australian Open) and the Victorian State championships.

Obviously, events of this magnitude required working committees of their own and it was my job to co-ordinate all of the details including sponsor contact, ticket sales, advertising, promotion, courts, grounds and facility preparation etc., etc., necessary for a successful tournament. Other major competitive events that were conducted included the Pennant competition mentioned earlier and the Country Carnival where representative best players from each of the fourteen country regions would compete for championship titles and the Metropolitan Championships that would do the same. In addition, schoolgirls' and schoolboys' championships, inter-regional championships, interstate matches were all part of what was provided for players to hone their skills.

Even back in the days before open tennis, sponsorship was of prime importance and in a small way was helping to promote the game. We were fortunate to have companies supporting our championship and training programs which allowed us to present our activities and objectives to the general public. It could be said that this was the opening for what we see in sponsorship today. Has it gone too far? Are the best players really worth the millions of dollars that they earn in such a short time (six or so years at the top)? After all we were treated to some of the greatest matches ever played when the players played for the love of the game. Have the endorsement deals reached a level of idiosyncrasy? One might say, the other big time sports have it, why not tennis?

It is a question that each person must answer for themselves, but for me it is another story.

It could be said that this was enough to do in one job, but there was still the direct individual membership of the Association. With four thousand members, all activities, policies and concerns had to be administered. These duties included control of the facilities such as a licensed bar and restaurant (of which I was the licensee), squash courts, tennis courts, a pro shop, social functions, catering, corporate tennis days, building, grounds and court maintenance, and so on, not to mention the office work.

All of this took a permanent staff of twenty-three dedicated employees and an additional seventy-five-plus part-time workers, during seasonal activities.

During my tenure, in addition to our regular tennis programs, we presented spectacular events in the stadium for the benefit of members, and to also provide supplemental income to the Association's finances. These included the Harlem Globetrotters, the Australian Ballet, the Ice Capades (*Holiday on Ice*), massed bands, pop concerts and a World Championship Bantamweight boxing title.

The boxing event was an interesting venture, not only for us but for the boxing fraternity as a whole. It is worthy of some comment here and an experience that I will never forget. The contenders were Australian aboriginal phenom star, Lionel Rose, holder of the title, against Alan Rudkin of Great Britain, who would take each other to the limit on stage, or should I say on court, in front of a worldwide televised audience. The date was fixed for Friday night, March 7th, 1969 and we went into action with this massive project.

The stadium courts, three magnificent grass, were to be converted into a boxing ring with trainer benches and all the paraphernalia that goes with them, and of course, ringside seats. The whole area would be covered with plywood, much like a jigsaw puzzle, to protect the surface, before the ring itself was constructed. The additional ringside seats would bring the spectator capacity to around fourteen and a half thousand, making it the biggest crowd ever to view a boxing match in Australian history. Obviously there was great concern about damage to our hallowed stadium courts but the contractors were very co-operative and agreed that they would not need to cover the arena more than three days in advance and that everything would be removed the day after the event. The details were infinite and time flew. One month before the match, there was not a seat to be had; it was a complete sellout. Things could not have been going smoother until ten days before our title fight when I received a call from a "water diviner" (a person who uses the forked stick method to determine where water is underground), who told me it was going to rain heavily on our Friday night spectacular. He told me that we should change our date to the Saturday when it would be a fine, pleasant evening. What did I have here? A nut case? Someone who was trying to undermine our efforts? Who was this person? Should I take him seriously? I had a thousand other questions. Well, the first thing to do was check him out.

It turned out that he was well respected in his home state of Queensland and that he had a ninety percent-plus rate of accuracy with his predictions. Water diviners play an important role in the Australian outback where drilling is impossible due to inaccessibility of conventional equipment. They walk with these "V"-shaped sticks in front of them, holding onto each prong and when water is present, the point dips to the ground with unbelievable force. It is not always accurate but on many occasions water has been found where it was not known to exist.

We were now faced with the decision whether to change the dates or not. Our executive officers were in shock; however, after a lengthy battering of the options we had, we made the change to Saturday, March 8th.

The result of the decision was enormous. With only about seven days to go, we had to advise fourteen and a half thousand spectators of the change of date; television had to be re-scheduled worldwide (thank heavens the local TV people did that); and a million other details had to be re-thought. I must say that the cooperation of the press, radio and television was outstanding. They made repeated announcements on a daily basis and internally we advised our members. The result was that I did not receive one complaint of anyone missing the event.

Friday night arrived and, true to the prediction of our friend in Queensland, it rained.

We would have been completely washed out in our outdoor stadium. Saturday morning dawned with brilliant sunshine which continued throughout the day and provided us with a spectacular evening.

I will never forget the waves of people coming down the main road from the train station, forty to fifty wide and ten rows deep at a time, cars lined up out of sight waiting to get into the parking lots, the music playing and the electric atmosphere in the air. Lionel Rose went fifteen hard-fought rounds, defeating Alan Rudkin to retain his title, and the event went down as one of the great boxing matches in history.

Twelve months earlier no one would have thought that tennis could provide such a perfect relationship with another sport, but time has shown us that we can work together.

The stadium courts were unharmed and soon ready for the hard-fought tennis matches to come.

Of course all of the other non-tennis events had their own elements of excitement and each of them was an experience unique to itself. I do not remember any of them being rained out and on one occasion *Holiday on Ice*, a fairytale skating extravaganza, played out again on our stadium courts converted to an ice rink, ran for twenty-one consecutive nights.

I must say that every member of the staff contributed greatly to my tennis experiences during my tenure at Kooyong and I will remember them fondly as friends as well as work mates.

Many people have asked me about the name Kooyong and its origin. It is an Australian aboriginal word meaning, "Haunt of the Wild Fowl."

In the early days, at the extreme end of the Association's property was a body of water that was fed by an underground spring, about the size of four tennis courts. This made an ideal spot for various species of fowl to come for food and water, and before urbanization, was a great hunting place for aborigines. They would stand like sticks, perfectly still with spear in hand, waiting patiently for the right moment, and with a sudden thrust, secure that fowl or odd fish, which would provide a succulent meal indeed. Even today, with the spring covered over with tennis courts, you can see the birds hovering over the area squawking about the way man has stolen their heritage.

Every day was a new experience at the Lawn Tennis Association of Victoria, much the same as a tennis match. One never knew what his opponent was going to serve up so one had to be versatile, flexible and prepared to respond to the task at hand. One of the amenities of the association was a world class dining room and catering service and much like a high standard restaurant, it required constant evaluation of food to be served, and its variety. I can remember on one occasion, a members' representative being upset that I spoke too often to the chef about the menu. My concern of course was to make sure that there was a varied selection of food for members to choose from and that their satisfaction was a top priority, when dining at the club. The same representative would have been just as upset if he did not have those choices. A membership of four thousand can keep one on his toes with little things like that.

With the introduction of Open tennis in 1968 the scene changed dramatically. Not so much from how the game itself was played, but by the players. The vast majority outside the professional circle continued on without change but in the "new" Open Championships we would eventually get to see more players from Asia, Europe and the United States bringing their vast array of new techniques and styles. It was a difficult time for Australian tennis because of our geographical location; and the lack of abundant prize money, so readily available in the U.S., made for a slow transition. It took some years before we could garner enough prize money to attract the caliber of player necessary to call it success. Today, Australia presents one of the best tournaments in the world in the Australian Open which is the first of the four Grand Slam events in the calendar year of tennis.

The tennis viewing public, however, was ready for Open tennis as was displayed in the 1959 professional tour organized by the founder of professional tennis, the great Jack Kramer. Kramer brought his team to Australia against opposition from the Lawn Tennis Association of Australia who refused him the use of their affiliate's facilities, which included us. Unperturbed, Kramer had a special court made that could be laid anywhere.

Known as "the court that Jack built," it was made of Resswood marine plywood and at that time was the only one of its kind in the world. Built in 45 sections and measuring 125 feet long and 63 feet wide it was raised 18 inches off the ground. Because of the necessity to transport it from city to city it was considered to be of light weight, weighing in at approximately 19 tons. An amazing fact was that there were no nails or screws in the whole area, and it maintained its rigidity. A special plastic paint known as Plastic Render was manufactured with a fine special grade of sand mixed in it, giving the players good footing, but prevented the ball from skidding.

Now that Kramer had a court that could be laid anywhere, and with the cooperation of groups like the Olympic Park Trust in Melbourne, he was able to erect his playing arena in the magnificent Olympic swimming stadium that had been built for the Olympic Games in 1956. The almost eight thousand seating capacity arena was packed every session with spectators eager to see the giants of that tennis era such as Pancho Gonzalez, Lew Hoad, Ken Rosewall, Tony Trabert, Frank Sedgman and Pancho Segura, do their thing. It would not be until 1963 that these great players were permitted to play at venues like Kooyong, when the Australian association lifted its ban, and capacity crowds of thirteen thousand were treated to first class thrilling performances.

Much like a general spectator, I did not have a feeling for how much pride, love and devotion goes into the preparation of a stadium center court that features a grass surface, until I joined the staff in 1966. Here I got my initiation. The grassed area of the arena at Kooyong could provide two playable courts at the same time separated by an unused singles court which became the "center court" for Championship and Davis Cup play.

Every blade of grass was manicured to perfection by the ground staff so as to provide the best playing surface for the players.

On special occasions, when ticket sales demanded it, the seating area of the stadium could be expanded to accommodate over twenty thousand fans (close in size to the U.S. Open Arthur Ashe stadium in New York today). It was a real experience to learn from these talented, behind-the-scenes craftsmen.

To be part of the excitement in administering and promoting events such as Davis Cup, the Australian Open Championships, the Victorian Open Championships, the two thousand strong Schoolgirls' and Schoolboys' Championships, the Country and Metropolitan Carnivals, the Pennant Competition, the Municipal Championships with over two thousand participants and the coaching classes for the most promising junior players in the State, as well as having a close relationship with every affiliated club and association, was indeed a truck load of experiences of their own, that can never be forgotten.

One particular happening was during the final weekend of the 1970 Victorian Open Championships. Semi-final day was on Saturday and at about lunch time, two hours before the first match, President Harry Hopman came to me and said, "I want you to take me to the airport."

I replied, "That is impossible, we have semi-finals to play."

His response, "Have your assistant handle it, we are leaving in an hour and I will explain on the way."

With much panic I got organized, and we left as planned. His simple statement to me was that he was going to the United States and would not be back. After the initial shock and nearly running off the road, I asked him who knew about this and who was taking over. He replied, "No one knows except you and when you get back tell Ian Carson (one of four vice-presidents) that he is acting president until the next election. I cannot tell you anything else now, but I will write you and Carson and explain everything."

Well, the shock waves reverberated around the Association when I got back with the news that almost over-shadowed the finals. Like a true stalwart, Ian Carson took over confidently, and was duly elected President at the next Annual General Meeting, later that year.

Perhaps the biggest of my experiences was to start in the early days of January 1972.

Kooyong was the host to the sixtieth Australian Championships, which was now an "Open" event and being played over the dates of December 26th, 1971 through January 3rd, 1972. Up until that time it was considered to be the most successful tennis tournament, excluding Davis Cup, ever played in Australia. Both attendances and gate takings had created new records.

As was the case with all major events, my working days produced long hours often starting at 6:30 A.M. and going past midnight. It was during this tournament that I received a telephone call that would change the life of my whole family.

In preparation for the upcoming semi-finals I had arrived at my office just after 6:30 in the morning and as I walked down the passageway, I could hear the telephone ringing. My thoughts were, "Hell, I can't even get into my office at this time of day without the phone dictating my first action." I dumped my bag, picked up the phone and said gruffly, "Aitchison."

A squeaky little voice said, "Alex, it's Harry here." In response, still in a bad frame of mind, I commented, "Harry who? You bloody fool, I know a dozen people named Harry."

The voice came back, "Hopman, who else, will you stop the nonsense, this call is costing money."

Needless to say, I was dumbfounded. I had received a brief note from him after he left for the U.S. but this was the first conversation we had had since 1970. I said, "Good God, when did you get into town?"

He replied, "I'm not in town, I'm in New York, will you please keep quiet, I have something to say."

He went on to tell me how he had become involved with the Port Washington Tennis Academy on Long Island and how the owner, Hy Zausner, was passionately pursuing his interest in providing the best junior teaching facility in the United States. At that time there were no academies as we know them today, only the individual coaches who could not handle the numbers wanting to learn the game, so there was a need for places where large groups of students could come to test their skills against each other. Zausner had three sons, none of whom were interested in his project and he had asked Hopman if he knew anyone that could do the job. The answer was "Yes, but I don't think you will get him."

Zausner responded, "How do you know if you don't ask?"

"So," said Hopman, getting back to our phone conversation, "Here we are, are you interested?" I told him I was always interested in bettering myself and with that he put the owner on the phone. At the end of our twenty-minute conversation I knew what this man wanted to do. His desire was to provide a place where aspiring young players could come and learn the art of being the best that they could be and to make available the many facets of the game that would enable them to reach lofty goals, if that was their desire. As a multi-millionaire he had the means to put all of this in place, but he needed someone with the knowledge to put it together. One of my frustrations in Australia was the lack of finances that would allow us to expand our junior programs.

I was so excited that I could have left right there and then but obviously many eventualities had to be considered. I was married with three children. I was happy with what I considered to be the best tennis job in Australia. What about schooling for my children, housing and the cost of living? What if it did not work out? These fears and more I presented to Hy Zausner and asked for answers to all of my questions. Of course, my wife Marjorie would have to be consulted also. Hy responded promptly within a few days and then at a later telephone conversation, when he was still holding my interest, he commented, "How much do you want and when can you come?" With an agreement that if it did not work out after twelve months, from either side, we would return to Australia, no hard feelings.

Our family got down to serious thinking and Marjorie and I mulled over all sides of the equation, and eventually decided to give it a try.

On April 27th, 1972 our family sailed on the Greek passenger liner, *The Ellinis*, for a well earned rest, the United States of America and a new experience.

8
Civil Defense

The tasks I had to perform in my years at the Lawn Tennis Association of Victoria were certainly onerous and varied, but I was not prepared for one presented to me in August of 1970. It came in the form of a letter, which I still have, that reads:

Mr. A. Aitcheson* Section   7
Kooyong Tennis Courts, Area   4b (Kooyong)
Glenferrie Rd. Date   3/8/70
Kooyong Our Ref.   0410E
Vic.

Dear Sir,

Civil Defence Programme

Under the direction of the Civil Defence, we are entering extensive training to organize both Civil and Industrial Companies for the purpose of the Fire Fighting in the event of danger from Nuclear raids.

As a citizen whose loyalty to the Government is unquestionable, we believe we may count on you as a patriot for full co-operation. We have therefore taken the liberty of appointing you Nuclear Warden for the division in which you reside.

Training will be confined to one night per week for the next six months, from 6–00 P.M. until 11–00 P.M.

Enclosed is a list of the various equipment required by you as Nuclear Warden of your district.

Yours faithfully,
R. Fallin
Chairman Civil Defence
Sub-Committee

*Spelling as written

Civil Defence Nuclear Warden
List of Equipment

1. Respirator.
2. Axe to carry in belt.
3. Stirrup pump to be carried over left shoulder.
4. Long household shovel to be carried on right shoulder.
5. Extension ladder to be carried under left arm.
6. Rake to be carried in left hand.
7. Scoop to be carried in right hand.
8. Whistle to be carried from mouth.
9. Belt to be worn around waist with 10 hooks for carrying sandbags and four pails of water.
10. Two wet blankets around neck.
11. Steel helmet with brim turned up to carry extra water.
12. Extra sand to be carried in all pockets.
13. Broom to be inserted in the only place available to the Warden to enable him to sweep the floors as he progresses.
14. Box of matches to light the bloody bomb if it doesn't go off.

I hope you get as much of a laugh out of this as I did.

9
Richard Alonzo "Pancho" Gonzalez

Pancho was born on May 9th, 1928 in Los Angeles, California. By the time he had reached twenty years of age, he had established himself as a contender to win many major world class tennis titles. During the Australian professional tour of 1959, we were to see and learn firsthand just how tough he could be as a player and as a personality.

No one can dispute his great talent on the court. Those who saw him play marveled at the ability of this giant to perform at the highest level of athleticism and apply pressure on his opponent while he was doing it. Even off the court, you got the feeling that he was applying that same pressure to someone or another. He had an aura all of his own.

In addition to the scheduled tour, I had organized additional stops at some of the major clubs in the state of Victoria. One case in particular was a high visibility grass court club at which Pancho was the featured player.

During the warm up, he approached the baseline umpire and said to him, "If you call anything out on me I will knock your f——n head off your shoulders." It just so happened that I was sitting immediately behind the linesman, who rose out of his chair, and at full height, had his head barely opposite Pancho's chest, and heard it all. The linesman calmly said, "Mr. Gonzalez, I am the president of this club and want you to know that you are here earning money at my pleasure. Please return to the court and do your thing and I will sit down, and do mine." There were no more episodes of intimidation during the match.

Later that evening, we were in the local milk bar getting drinks, before we went on to the next town, where Pancho ordered a milkshake with five scoops of ice cream in it. As the scoops were small, he wanted to get the full flavor. Somehow the server got the order wrong (was this more intimidation?) shortchanging him on the number of ice creams. After one gulp, Pancho slammed the canister down on the counter and swished milk shake everywhere, screaming, "You couldn't get the ice cream right, could you?" In a rage he stamped out of the store.

One learned not to argue with this man when he was in such a mood, and never ever when he took up his travel position in our station wagon, which was the whole of the passenger side from front to back, on top of the luggage, so he could sleep while we traveled to our next venue.

10
Coming to America

Not long after we had said goodbye to family and friends, we went to our cabin to unpack and prepare for our long trip over the ocean to the other side of the world. It would take us just about four weeks. As was customary, each passenger was allowed cabin baggage which was available for a daily change of clothes, further baggage that was accessible from a holding area that would see you through the trip, and the rest of your belongings were in the main hold and not procurable until the journey was over. Going through the bags that had been placed in our cabin prior to boarding, I could not find my belongings. They were just not there. I assumed that they had been put in the accessible area, but on inquiry, they were not there either.

A search by the crew in charge failed to find the missing bags. This was great; here I was with just the clothes I had on and the uncertainty of when I could change again. The search would go on to no avail and my wardrobe would be added to at each port of call with new purchases. On arrival at our final destination, they were in fact found in the main hold, and I finished up with a second set of clothes that eventually was paid for by the insurance coverage I had taken out.

Our journey took us from our home town of Melbourne via the bustling metropolis of Sydney to the pristine pastures of New Zealand, where there are more sheep than people, to the island of Tahiti where the ship berthed, overlooking the main street. Next stop, the Panama Canal, with the great locks connecting the different levels of the Caribbean Sea and the Pacific Ocean. What an experience to see these massive ocean liners looking like toy boats in a bathtub as your ship rises to incredible heights of water elevation and you look down at one going the other way. Truly a remarkable feat of human ingenuity.

Curaçao was our last stop before reaching the United States, and it is hard to explain the oppressive humidity prevalent in that part of the world. The moment you are exposed to the outside air it is literally like taking a shower with your clothes on.

I found the custom of honoring the sacred goats fascinating on this island. Here they have right-of-way, access to buildings, back yards, front yards, fields and anywhere they want to go, without fear.

We had almost concluded our journey, had celebrated a birthday for Marjorie, were honored with a dinner at the Captain's table because of our mutual interest in Greek tennis players, enjoyed the participation of our children in fancy dress parties, went through the sea-sickness process, relaxed on deck for bouillon every morning and did justice to the magnificent food that was offered day and night. We were now relaxed and ready for what was to come.

On May 26th, 1972, *The Ellinis* sailed into New York harbor and our almost four-week journey from Australia was over. It was at sunrise, and passengers had been advised that we would sail past the Statue of Liberty, which is the symbol of freedom for Americans, and we were encouraged to go topside to view the scene. If you have never seen Lady Liberty at sunrise, you have missed one of the most spectacular and touching sights that you can imagine. Here she was, holding her torch up high in the red glow that only mother nature at sunrise can paint, welcoming visitors from other lands to her shores. For a few moments it was as if time had stood still just for us, and the expectation of what was to come pounded away at our hearts.

We docked on the west side of Manhattan where the mighty Hudson River provided our berthing place. It was truly amazing how this giant three-thousand- passenger liner glided slowly into her berth without a bump. Looking down from the deck and seeing the multitude of people waiting to greet their loved ones and friends was indeed a sight not to be forgotten. Somewhere down there, among this throng, was the beginning of this new venture.

After going through customs and immigration, which seemed to take forever, we were met by my longtime friend Harry Hopman and his wife Lucy, and to make sure that we had enough transportation for our belongings, Joe, the head maintenance man from the Academy, was there with his pick-up truck.

After our greetings we set off for our destination, our three sons with Joe, and we marveled at the maze of highways and the volume of traffic both vehicular and pedestrian. We were really in the big time now. Until you see New York for the first time you cannot imagine the enormity of the city and its environs.

Our journey took us about an hour, arriving at lunchtime, when we met my new boss Hy Zausner, his wife Annabel and all of the staff.

The reality of our decision to come half way around the world suddenly had arrived, and for me it was to become the tennis experience of my lifetime.

11
The Port Washington Tennis Academy

The Port Washington Tennis Academy, or "Port" as it was lovingly known, was often referred to by players from all over the world as a place that if you had not been there, you had not had the full tennis experience. Situated in the town of Port Washington, Long Island, New York, it opened its doors in 1966 to literally thousands of players from every part of the globe. Catering to all ability levels from beginners to touring professionals, it provided the opportunity for every player to hone their skills and reach the goals they had set for themselves. It was the first major tennis learning academy to be created in the United States at the beginning of the so-called boom years.

Just thirty minutes away from the famed Forest Hills stadium and New York's two major airports, John F. Kennedy and LaGuardia, it was ideally situated as a stopover facility for practice when top players were competing in the area.

It had its beginning in 1966 when Hy Zausner, a philanthropist with a burning desire to help young people, opened the doors to all comers. Zausner had tried other means to achieve his desire including day camps, the scout movement and even considered building a drug rehabilitation center. However, he was on vacation in Puerto Rico when he noticed the resort tennis professional giving a lesson. As a handball player he had a good concept of ground strokes, hitting the ball in the air and footwork combined with speed and balance. However, the serve was completely different so he decided to get some serving lessons. When the pro learned that his new student had not played tennis before, he wanted to start with ground strokes, but on Zausner's insistence, not giving the pro any options, the serving lessons started. After a daily series at this component of the game, he quickly learned the basics and on his return to Long Island came to the realization that his concern for young people and his newly discovered love for tennis, were destined to form an inevitable merger.

Work began almost immediately and two courts were built on a parcel of reclaimed land that he owned, with a small hut on the property acting as a clubhouse. Zausner got the word out that lessons were available and soon prospective students started to make inquiries. Adult friends were invited to join as members who helped to provide a cash flow and soon the need for a teaching staff became a real necessity. None of Zausner's three sons were interested, so he had the idea of calling the pro in Puerto Rico who had taught him how to serve. He presented him with the problem along with an invitation to teach and help set up a program. An agreement was made and Nick Bollettieri, the same world famous coach of today, played an important role in the initial formation of the academy. At that time Bollettieri, who had not yet reached his present status, was anxious to start his own facility, but Zausner was adamant that his place would never carry a personal name, and that forever it would be known as the Port Washington Tennis Academy. The relationship ended on a friendly basis and the search was on again for a high profile professional. The numbers of students had increased considerably, and the better junior players had a need for advanced coaching.

At the U.S. Open in September of 1970, Hy Zausner met Harry Hopman who earlier that year had moved to the United States from Australia and offered him the position of Director of his Junior Program. His acceptance and expertise went a long way to putting "Port" into the world class teaching arena. He would stay there until he opened his own Harry Hopman's International Tennis training facility in Largo, Florida in 1976.

As the academy grew in student numbers so did the need for more courts, and it seemed like construction was a never-ending process. On my arrival in 1972 the facility now boasted six permanent indoor courts, five outdoor clay courts, which were covered by two bubbles in the winter months, and six permanent outdoor hard courts. Eventually, the five bubbled ones were covered with a permanent building and extended to seven playing arenas, with viewing for spectators. The building also housed a gymnasium, a study hall, a video room, an office for the production of a college and junior tennis magazine, designed to help juniors in their applications to college, and storage.

In addition, the academy was now established as a 501(C) 3 non-profit charitable institution, aimed primarily at developing junior tennis players. This status from the Internal Revenue Service allowed the academy to operate on a tax-exempt basis, thus providing additional funds to be poured back into the program. Eventually, the academy gained real estate tax-exemption as well, solidifying its existence.

"Port" gained a worldwide reputation mainly through John McEnroe, its most distinguished alumnus, as well as his doubles partners Peter Fleming, Vitas Gerulaitis, and Mary Carillo, to name a few. The academy was extremely proud of the heavy representation it had in the main draws of Wimbledon and the U.S. Open. In 1978 six Port Washingtonians competed at Wimbledon and in 1980, thirteen alumni played in the main draw of the U.S. Open. John Parsons, the esteemed British tennis writer, called it a Rocket Base like Cape Canaveral, where potential American stars were launched into the future.

Despite the output of champions and the slogan in the lobby that said, "Tennis isn't a matter of life and death, it's more important than that," the Port Washington Tennis Academy was not an assembly line. Although there was an intensity of training and a healthy emphasis on discipline (from strict nonsmoking rules, to enforcement of sportsmanship on court), the goal was not necessarily to produce champions, but to develop the participants' potential as players, and as young men and women to the fullest.

Our mandate was that if championship potential was observed, we would do all that we could to develop that potential to its maximum extent. However, the essential aspect was that students should derive from the program as much enjoyment as possible while honing their skills. Nevertheless, our staff of twenty dedicated coaches, was deadly serious about bringing out the championship potential of those who chose to make tennis their career. Tournament play was an integral part of training, and we provided about 150 of these each year catering to every level from novice to international ranking categories. Some events were training exercises to prepare juniors for the tournament scene, and others provided United States Tennis Association and International Tennis Federation sanctioned play for the serious player. Matches against college varsity teams and inter-club games with other leading tennis facilities were arranged for selected team players within the program and occasionally, overseas competition would be on the agenda. When a student reached graduation, we were there to help, and over the years hundreds of "Port" students obtained tennis scholarships at leading colleges throughout the nation.

The heart of the program though was the individualized instruction. The plan was to have three students per coach, but never more than four; and instructional classes were divided into nine ability levels. This allowed students to progress at their own level with the ability to move up as their skills demanded. Training did not end, though, when the lesson was over. The academy provided extras not usually found in other teaching facilities like a fully equipped gym for strengthening bodies and increasing stamina, videotaping to spot weaknesses and flaws in strokes, closed circuit TV on each court, enabling coaches and parents to look in on a student, a well stocked library of tennis manuals and other books on sports and fitness, and a whirlpool and steam room to ease those aching bodies. If medical treatment or advice on sports injuries and/or illnesses were needed, this was provided by some of the nation's most qualified physicians headed by Dr. Irving Glick (then chairman of the U.S. Open medical team), and Dr. Gary Wadler.

Additionally, there was our voluntary "training for life" program, providing a general library, a study hall, a TV viewing room and chess tables, all of which enhanced concentration, so important in tennis.

I think it is important to note that players came from all over the world to participate in our training programs that were used as rungs on the ladder of tennis success. Although the vast majority were from the United States many came from Europe, Asia, the Middle East, the African nations and Australia to hone their skills in their personal endeavors.

Port Washington was also famous for the snacks it dispensed to students at no cost.

Not too many people realized that providing cookies,

bananas, soup, soda, hot chocolate, tea, milk and coffee was more than a goodwill gesture. It was part of the philosophy of treating all students alike. If there had been a charge, the student who could not afford to pay would have had to go without. A sense of inequality and insecurity would take root, and only those who had the money could snack away to their hearts' content.

It was also our policy to award scholarships to serious minded juniors who could not afford to pay for their classes. These were never awarded on the basis of ability, but on financial need only and the family's ability to pay.

So that the academy could always be kept in the forefront of the tennis scene, our executive officers sat on many committees of the United States Tennis Association and the Eastern Tennis Association, giving immeasurable volunteer hours to the game of tennis, in its development throughout the nation.

After fourteen years of experiences at the "Port," most of which have not been told here because they are too many; I have learnt that the positive things are those that we should cherish. The important thing to know is what this great facility offered to students and players alike in the early days of tennis growth, and I have tried to do this here. I can never express the pleasure gained by meeting the people that I met from all over the world, the events we conducted, and the thousands of young people that we helped.

If it were not for the vision, the willingness to spend his own money, often in the hundreds of thousands of dollars annually, subsidizing the operation, and the inexhaustible dedication to helping juniors, I would never have met Hy Zausner and worked by his side.

It was with great sadness that my tenure there came to an end when Hy became too ill to control the continuing outcome of the academy. The return of one of his sons had brought back the old saying that "blood is thicker than water" and I learned this the hard way. Although my agreement was that I could stay for the rest of my life, there was a strong feeling that I was a threat to the heritage of the returnee. Nothing could have been further from the truth, as my sole purpose was to carry out the wishes of this man who had given so much to the game of tennis. Resignation was my only option after being accused of actions that were the figments of imagination.

12
John McEnroe

I first met John in 1971 when he came to Australia as part of a junior team that Harry Hopman had organized in conjunction with American Airlines and their inaugural flight to Down Under. John was 12 years old at the time and even then the signs of the great player that he became, were showing through. Little did I know at this meeting that eventually I would have a lot to do with this young man, because at that stage of my career I had no idea that I would be relocating to the United States, let alone managing the facility where he played and trained.

In September of 1973, eighteen months after I assumed the role of manager of the Port Washington Tennis Academy on Long Island, New York, John was showing a great deal of promise, being ranked number 6 nationally in 14 and under singles and number 1 in national 14 and under doubles. He was starting to be recognized as a real potential in the world of junior tennis. As such, it was my pleasure to recommend him for inclusion to the Wilson Sporting Goods Company free list for tennis players, on which he was duly placed.

I look back on those days and remember that John McEnroe was feisty then and definitely had a mind of his own.

One particular incident that was being observed from

my office window by Hopman and myself, showed John missing an easy volley at the net. He was so incensed at his mistake, that he ran to the back fence of the outdoor court that he was playing on, clawed at the fence and smashed his racket in disgust. With emotion showing in his eyes, he went to his bag at the side of the court, got out another racket, and returned to play as if nothing had happened.

I was not about to report him to his newly found supplier of equipment, but as tournament director it was time for me to intervene and tell him that his behavior was unacceptable. I turned to leave my office and proceed to the court when a grip like a vise clamped down on my shoulder and the voice of the owner, Harry Hopman, said, "Where are you going?"

I said, "I am going to talk to John about his court manners."

Hopman replied, "Leave him alone, he is my responsibility." I argued that the matter needed to be attended to now, but he insisted that he would deal with it. Reluctantly I conceded but I was not happy. Incidents like that needed to be dealt with on the spot if young players were to learn how to conduct themselves on the court.

After the match, Hopman called John into his office and said to him, "What was all that nonsense about?" John, who could not look anyone in the eye (and today still cannot), simply said, "I lost my cool." The response from Hopman was, "Well, don't let it happen again." And John left.

What a turnaround I was seeing from the man whose reputation had branded him as possibly the toughest disciplinarian the game of tennis had ever seen.

Well, in my opinion things did not improve with John's attitude or his demeanor over the years and he maintained his image as one who did not like the system, irrespective of whether it was right or not, and was going to do things his way.

As an example, he would arrive for his training program right on time and demand to start immediately, giving no consideration to the fact that someone else might have been on the court before him. Likewise, when the lesson was over, he was gone. No extracurricular activity for him such as weight training, video replay, discussion, etc.

Additionally, when we played matches against IV league colleges, John was never around when it was time to leave. He would be found on the basketball court or fraternizing with other students. Someone always had to look for him.

The worst incident concerning John took place at the Concord Hotel in upstate New York in 1976 where he and three other players from the Port Washington Tennis Academy were playing in an invitational junior tournament. Contrary to John's father making a statement that they were not representing "Port," the Academy had been given four spots in the draw to fill with our representatives. Surely that gave those players an obligation to represent us in a proper manner.

The incident occurred when John and his doubles partner at the time, Peter Rennert, went over the line of "youthful enthusiasm" as his father later explained their actions to me.

In Richard Evans' book titled *McEnroe: A Rage for Perfection,* John admitted that it was a schoolboy prank that got out of hand. It was established that John and a friend, Peter Rennert, decided to have some "fun" by throwing a lighted towel into the girls' dormitory. The prank was to cause pandemonium as John yelled "fire" and Peter rushed into the room spraying water in all directions. It would be some years later, when John was a more mature person, that he admitted to being a part of a dangerous and irresponsible act. Peter Rennert, however, never conceded his position.

I put this to you, the reader:

a. The incident took place in the older section of the hotel where there was no sprinkler system, just water buckets and sand.
b. That area was of wooden structure.
c. There were three thousand guests in the hotel at the time.
d. This "schoolboy prank" that got out of hand, the actions of seventeen-year-olds, could have cost many people their lives.
e. Were we right to take the action of suspension as a disciplinary measure?
f. Maybe, just maybe, if tighter control and better parental guidance had been applied, these young men might have acted like normal human beings, and this situation never would have arisen.

None of the above takes away from the great talent that John McEnroe has shown the world in mastering the game of tennis. I have the greatest respect for his achievements, and he has been a great champion. I just wish he could have done it like his idol Rod Laver.

13
Irving V. Glick, M.D.: A Friend Indeed

I have been blessed over the years to have made many friends (and some enemies as well), but one man stands out from the crowd and deserves my undying gratitude for his willingness to help his fellow man. His name, Dr. Irving Glick. It is not my intention to write an epistle on various people in this book, but there are a few who have contributed greatly to my tennis experience, and Dr. Glick is one of them.

As I mentioned earlier, I came with my family from Australia in 1972 to manage the Port Washington Tennis Academy on Long Island, New York. Dr. Glick, an avid tennis aficionado, played at the academy and shared his love of the game with all those who came in contact with him. One of the great gifts he gave to others was in providing medical service to all players from every part of the world who visited Port (the academy nickname), free of charge. Eventually, he gave so much of his time to helping others there, that it was necessary, and my pleasure, to provide him with an office at our facility.

On a personal note, I can never repay him for the love, devotion and attention that he bestowed on my whole family during my tenure, let alone the financial relief that he was responsible for on our behalf. Even today as I write, from the confinement of his chair, due to ill health, a call to him always ignites his first question, "Can I do anything for you?"

It was a great privilege for me to work with this man on many occasions relating to the well-being of tennis players, where his knowledge and expertise was shared willingly, and aided me in my task of administration.

A summary of his untold history is as follows.

He graduated from the prestigious Stuyvesant High School in New York in the early 1930s. At a time when the United States was suffering from the Great Depression, he attended Baylor University in Waco, Texas, where he received a B.A. degree, in 1936. After graduating, he returned to New York and attended New York University. He then attended the University of Maryland Medical School, obtaining a medical degree in 1940.

Following his graduation, he held internships and successive residencies at Mt. Sinai, Bellevue, Harlem and Montefiore Hospitals, in New York.

In 1944, during the Second World War he entered the medical corps of the U.S. military with the rank of Major, and was assigned as an orthopedic surgeon to various military hospitals. During this period he was among the first to use bone grafting in reconstructive surgery. Because of his specialty and the urgent and continuing needs of wounded soldiers, he and certain other physicians were retained or "frozen" in the military beyond the end or cessation of the war. Dr. Glick's last assignment in the military was at Oliver General Hospital in Augusta, Georgia, a large orthopedic and psychiatric installation. While stationed at Oliver, he met and subsequently married Tommie Wurtsbaugh, an American Red Cross psychiatric social worker, in 1947.

After discharge from the Army in 1947 Dr. Glick returned to New York City and continued specialized training at Mt. Sinai and Bellevue Hospitals. He then opened a private practice in New York City but continued his association with Mt. Sinai and Bellevue, as attending physician. During this period he joined the faculty of New York University Bellevue Medical Center as Professor of Orthopedic Surgery, where he taught for over twenty-five years. After living in New York for several years, Dr. Glick and his wife, for personal reasons as well as for their interest in tennis, moved to Great Neck, Long Island, and eventually set up his office there as well. He was one of the first physicians to work toward the establishment of the North Shore Community Hospital, and being increasingly aware of the need for medical care in the field of sports, he became one of the pioneers in the development of Sports Medicine.

At this time, Dr. Glick was physician for the Port Washington Tennis Academy and the Medical Director of the U.S. Open Tennis Championships, then held at the West Side Tennis Club in Forest Hills, Queens, Long Island, N.Y. In 1978 the United States Tennis Association moved the Open to a new stadium in Flushing, New York, at which time Dr. Glick established the medical department for the U.S. Open. His service to those championships spanned over twenty-five years. He has continued his interest and involvement with the United States Tennis Association as Honorary Chairman of the U.S.T.A. Sports Science Committee, and as Tournament Physician Emeritus of the U.S. Open.

His dedication to providing excellence in medical care to the tennis players, the public attending the games, and the staff of the U.S. Open, did not end there. His expertise extended also to football and basketball players as well.

In the 1970s, after working with coach Lou Carnesecca and the New Jersey Nets, he became associated with the St. John's basketball team, continuing to work with coach

Carnesecca. Carnesecca's interest in a player's progress, health, total development and welfare, present and future, as a role of the coaching staff (a philosophy also reflected by the University), was an approach shared by Dr. Glick as well. This led to a remarkable, unique and satisfying association with the "Red Storm" basketball team for over twenty years, until Dr. Glick retired in 1999.

Dr. Glick was always reluctant to speak about himself, and today still tends to minimize his great contributions. Even now, when we think of the pressures, daily traumas and negative influences that our young people are faced with as they grow up, it is a good thing to know of another's story, especially when it is that of a young student who overcame obstacles, loved learning, persevered, and achieved the goals that he had set for himself.

I know that he has had many heartwarming experiences in his long and productive career, and countless tributes from grateful patients, friends, tennis players, basketball players, football players and sports people in general, but the most unique, was the public tribute that was televised nationally in his honor at the 1999 U.S. Open Tennis Championships on September 3rd of that year, before a capacity crowd of twenty thousand plus.

The tribute was as follows:

Tonight we are giving special recognition to Dr. Irving Glick. Dr. Glick was the Medical Director of the U.S. Open Tennis Championships from 1970 through 1991 and has since been the tournament Physician Emeritus. Dr. Glick has been a pioneer in modern day sports medicine. He laid the groundwork for the high standard of medical care that everyone receives at the Open. He founded the U.S.T.A. Sports Medicine Committee, and was instrumental in shaping the U.S.T.A. and International Tennis Federation drug-testing programs. He is universally recognized as a physician with exceptional clinical skills and judgment, and even more as a compassionate gentleman. For his pioneering efforts and unique contributions to medicine and sports, Dr. Glick has received numerous awards, including induction into St. John's University Sports Hall of Fame, induction into the Eastern/U.S.T.A. Tennis Hall of Fame and recipient of the International Tennis Hall of Fame's Tennis Educational Merit Award.

The U.S. Open is privileged to have Dr. Glick as a family member.

Dr. Glick and his wife Tommie have two children, John and Lisabeth and three grandchildren, Lauren, Jennifer and Brian.

What a great privilege, honor and experience for me to be associated with such a man, who saved the lives of so many of our wounded soldiers in wartime, and gave so unselfishly to all he came in contact with during his career.

14
The Eastern Tennis Association

The day we arrived in New York was the day that I was introduced to the Eastern Tennis Association (E.T.A.). On arrival at the Port Washington Tennis Academy there was a large junior tournament being played and volunteers from the E.T.A. were in charge of scheduling and putting matches on. I met with these people and gained some information about how things were done in the United States. Some events like this one—the Memorial Day Weekend Championships—were actually run by volunteers from the E.T.A. in order to take the administrative burden away from the staff of these facilities that provided their courts and amenities. I soon learned that the Port Washington Tennis Academy was a stalwart supporter of E.T.A. events and it was not long before running some of these tournaments became my responsibility. With the policy of the academy to provide every opportunity for juniors to achieve their goals on the court, it became a strong part of the program there to sponsor numerous competitive events for all ages and levels of play. The East was indeed fortunate to have such a force promoting their objectives.

I became very involved in the junior aspect of the Eastern Tennis Association and eventually was invited to join their junior affairs committee. With the blessing of my boss, I accepted, and joined others in the policy-making goals of the association with respect to juniors, rules of play, rankings etc. In 1975 I was appointed co-chairman of that committee and in 1976, the overall responsibility of chairman. Shortly after, in a re-organization program, the committee became the Junior Tennis Council, and we set about governing our section (one of seventeen making up the United States Tennis Association), in a way that would provide equality to all players in their pursuits.

Rankings, which incidentally started in the 1920s, were of particular concern because of the growth of the game, and the pressure that was being brought to bear on junior players to perform by their parents and coaches. I had numerous discussions with them about priorities such as growing up and education, and had to counsel many nine and ten year olds who were thinking about how much money they would make in the future, instead of learning the skills of the game, and having fun doing it. At one point I was involved with the United States Tennis Association and the International Tennis Federation in a study on burn-out in young players, and that led to the non ranking of ten and twelve year olds in the U.S., and the withdrawal of twelve and under play by the I.T.F. on an international basis.

Applying the rules in a fair way to everyone was also difficult at times. The first rule was that they (the rules) were not meant to punish, but were there to provide equality for all players. One such rule was that to be eligible for selection to National Championships, you had to play a minimum of four E.T.A. sanctioned tournaments from October 1st of the previous year. Based on performance at these tournaments and other results and rankings, a player would be endorsed to compete at the national events. It should be noted that the U.S.T.A. allocated quotas to each of the sections. Spots were limited in the draws and eagerly sought after by the players.

One young lady, Caroline Stoll, who was an outstanding player and a very nice person, decided in her wisdom (or that of her advisers), to play only three of the four necessary sanctioned events in the East, and played elsewhere to gain more tournament experience and competition. When the time came for endorsement I had to determine her ineligible because of her inability to comply with the rules. There was no doubt about her quality of play, and she probably would have been number one on our list. She was so upset that she decided to sue me, the Eastern Tennis Association and the United States Tennis Association.

I learned about the lawsuit while on vacation, and had to convey my testimony from a public phone booth in one-hundred-degree heat. The judge took one look at the rule and dismissed the case. The Jimmy Arias family were also considering a lawsuit under similar conditions but did not pursue the matter, after hearing the Stoll case decision.

Another junior conflict arose in 1982 during my presidential term, this time with the organizers of the Easter Bowl Junior Championships. The Easter Bowl, a very prestigious event for 18, 16 and 14 and under girls and boys, had been conducting these championships for years in the East, unopposed by other clubs because of its high visibility. In that year the director and committee decided to move the tournament to Florida, nearly thirteen hundred miles from the original site. This left a void in the Northeast for a major event. The Port Washington Tennis Academy, consistent with their policy of providing competition for all ages, added 14, 16 and 18 age groups to already established 10- and 12-year-old segments, under the title of the Puma Easter Classic.

There was a hue and cry from the Easter Bowl people about stealing their thunder, and as I was also employed by Port Washington T.A., I was naturally accused of having a conflict of interest. There were two good reasons why I had no conflict. First, the Puma Championship had to be sanctioned by the appropriate committee, which it was—not by me—and second, the Easter Bowl catered to about 300 players when there were over 89,000 registered juniors with the U.S.T.A. that year, nationwide. Surely there was enough room for two major tournaments at the same time, given their distance apart.

In addition, the dates of play for the divisions concerned were staggered five days apart in favor of the Easter Bowl so that if a player had entered both tournaments and was still competing in Florida when the Puma Classic commenced, they would withdraw from New York and Puma would be the loser.

It was my great desire to serve the two years of my Eastern presidency in a way that would be beneficial to all clubs and their members, and I called on my critics to reflect on their paranoia, and join me in helping to make tennis the game for a lifetime.

Although some experiences are not pleasant, there are many more that are. They both go with the territory and you learn to cope with the bad and savor the good.

Not long after our arrival in the U.S. I was looking for some tournament competition, and was amazed at the lack of club play, as I knew it from Australia. Not to say that it was not there, I just had not found it yet. I became aware of the Eastern Hard-Court Championships that was being played at a club not too far from where I worked, and decided to enter. The tournament committee did not know "this guy from Australia." How good is he? Should he be seeded? Well, I guess on the premise of being Australian, they thought that I could not be too bad, and was seeded number 5. I had no idea what that meant, as I did not know the caliber of play for this event. I managed to reach the quarter finals and was to meet Bill Johns, my opponent, the number 4 seed. I recall that it was a very windy day, which did not bother me, because an old saying is, "the wind starts in Australia," and we were taught to use the wind to our advantage in our basic learning process.

I won the first set 6–3 and was leading 3–0 in the second. On the change-over Bill was distraught with the wind, so we had a discussion. I gave him some pointers about playing in the wind, and found out that he was an excellent student. He came from behind to take the second set 6–4 and the third 6–3 to wrap up the match. After all my years of play, I finally learned the lesson not to help my opponent beat me. He was a heck of a nice guy though and later in 1977 we met again in the 45 and over division where I got my revenge by winning 6–3, 5–7, 7–5.

As my duties at the Port Washington Tennis Academy became more demanding I played less in local competition, but was delighted to be ranked in the East at number 4 in men's 45s and number 12 in men's 50s.

In 1978 I became vice-president of the Eastern Tennis Association and held that position until 1982, when I assumed the presidency. This position was for a two-year term as provided for by the constitution. During those six years I was still very involved with the junior process and actually delayed my term as president for two years to complete some of the programs that I was involved in. Of course there was the adult segment of the association, the day-by-day administration, the many in-and-out-of-state events, representation with other organizations, and the liaison necessary to service almost twenty thousand members that made up the affiliated clubs and associations in the various regions and districts.

Some of the excitement, but not all, was the provision of

a "caravan" coaching program, where a team of our teaching professionals would go out into the field and provide instruction to those players interested in the game who were financially less fortunate, and could not afford to pay for lessons.

Another was the Maureen Connolly Brinker Cup, an international competition for junior girls between the United States and Australia, at which I was pleased to be a committee member.

An attempt by me to form a junior umpires association, where juniors would officiate at junior events for their peers, unfortunately did not get off the ground as a completed project. I still think it is a great idea.

Yet another was the promotion and worldwide release of the movie *Players* starring Ali MacGraw and Dean-Paul Martin. The great Arthur Ashe and former champion Bill Talbert, then director of the U.S. Open, were the co-chairmen of this classic tennis movie which was screened at the Loews State Theater in New York on June 6th, 1979, followed by a party at the famed Studio 54. The proceeds from the event were forwarded to the Eastern Youth Tennis Foundation to support them in their work.

In 1982 and 1983 it was my privilege to present a tennis tournament seminar at the U.S.T.A. teachers conference in New York where all the nuts and bolts of how to run a tournament, and what you have to have and do to fulfill your mission, were explained.

Although my memory is filled with experiences, perhaps the greatest and certainly the most exciting, was being inducted into the Eastern Tennis Hall of Fame at the United Nations on April 19th, 2002. This honor, bestowed for services to tennis in the East, is indeed one that will be cherished by me for a lifetime. To join such legends as Paul Annacone, Arthur Ashe, Don Budge, Mary Carillo, Sarah

Palfrey Danzig, Peter Fleming, Vitas Gerulaitis, Althea Gibson, Carol Graebner, Ron Holmberg, Kathleen Horvath, Gene Mayer, John McEnroe, Ham Richardson, Dick Savitt and Bill Talbert, to name a few, is an experience that cannot be described.

To my friend Doris Herrick (herself a Hall of Famer in 2000), who was the executive director of the association throughout my years of service, thank you, Doris, for making my task possible.

Today I still serve on the board of directors of the Eastern Tennis Association, now called U.S.T.A. Eastern, and continue to learn more about our great game as it grows.

15
The Rolex International Junior Tennis Championships

It all began one day in 1976 when Beatrice Puton, wife of Roland Puton, then executive vice president of Rolex USA, called into the Port Washington Tennis Academy looking to buy a tennis racquet as a birthday present for her husband. Mrs. Puton, who knew exactly what she wanted, said to me, "My husband is a fanatical tennis player and I know that he wants a Dunlop Maxply racquet with a four and five eight grip. Do you have one?" As it happened, we did not have one in stock, but I said to her, "I can get one for you, when do you need it by?"

She needed it within a few days, and I promised to have it for her. During our conversation I inquired, "What does your husband do professionally, and how often does he play?" to which she replied, "He is the executive vice president of Rolex Watch USA, and he plays four or five times a week." I learned that they lived not far from the academy and told her I would call as soon as the racquet was ready.

At that time I was the chief executive officer of "Port" and when I met Mrs. Puton something clicked in my mind. This was the time when there was a strong need for an international junior tournament in the New York area, as the Orange Bowl, played in Florida, was the only Junior Davis Cup caliber event in the country. However, the Orange Bowl catered primarily to overseas juniors who came to play in the Continental and Sunshine Cup team matches, leading up to their tournament. When the Orange Bowl was over, there was a void in playing time that could be filled with another world class championship, and an opportunity to create a "junior circuit." As an event of this magnitude would need a sponsor, perhaps Rolex might be interested. When Mrs. Puton picked up the birthday gift, I told her of my thoughts and said, "Would you have your husband call me if he is interested in discussing my plan." In a matter of days, Roland Puton called and accepted an invitation for himself and his company president, René Dentan, to play tennis at the Port Washington Tennis Academy, where hopefully the event would be played, with our owner Hy Zausner and myself.

From the ensuing doubles game between us four executives, a partnership between Rolex and the PWTA was born. I had laid out the potential program, about which they showed great interest, and the obvious question; "How much is it going to cost?"

I replied; "I do not know, we are simply going to have to feel our way and see where it leads us. We, however, are prepared to meet the challenge in providing this event for the youth of the world."

After a short debate with each other, Roland Puton on behalf of Rolex said, "We will invest twenty thousand dollars in this wonderful venture and at its conclusion, re-evaluate for its future. Let's shake hands on that."

We were in a new business, plans were made, wheels began to spin, invitations were sent out, Port Washington geared up, and at Christmas 1977 the first Rolex International Junior Tennis Championships were staged. That first year juniors from thirty nations came, from kids hardly bigger than their racquets, to muscular 18-year-olds. They were 750 strong including a couple of very promising youngsters by the names of Ivan Lendl and Yannick Noah. So strong was the field that neither Ivan, or Yannick, were able to take any laurels home. The tournament continued to grow to the point where the numbers of contestants reached over 1,000, and the number of countries represented in any one year was 47. All told, over 60 nations competed in the Rolex Championships during the time that I was tournament director. It was the largest junior championship in the world until Rolex moved their sponsorship in 1987, due to me leaving Port Washington.

The list of graduates who moved into the pro ranks from this event, is mind boggling. Even though some of them did not win titles, nevertheless, many of them went on to great careers as world class players. Names like Louise Allen, Jimmy Arias, Pablo Arraya, Tracy Austin, Elise Burgin, Francesco Cancellotti, Johan Carlsson, Pam Casale, Scott Davis, Stefan Edberg, Kathleen Horvath, Per Hjerquist, Andrea Jaeger, Eric Korita, Ivan Lendl, Hana Mandlikova, Glen Michibata, Yannik Noah, Joakim Nystrom, Goran Prpec, Pam Shriver, Hana Strachonova, Henrik Sundstrom and Mats Wilander, are just a few.

The Rolex sponsorship provided in part, some monies that were allocated to visiting nations to help defray their travel costs, but the main burden belonged to the academy. The players were picked up from the airports, and transported to hotels where they were accommodated during the tournament. Bus transportation was then provided to and from the academy for matches. Breakfast, lunch and dinner were provided on a complimentary basis for all players and coaches. Also available during the championships, were some twenty-five thousand bananas, thirty thousand cookies and hundreds of gallons of milk and orange juice, all free for the taking. In non-match time, computer games, chess, checkers, television and live entertainment were part of the activities. The tournament logistics were a nightmare, with a hundred or so matches being scheduled daily in the early stages of the tournament. Staff was on duty from 6 A.M. each day and would rarely get away before midnight. Despite the crush and pressure, the lack of sleep, the loss of memory of when you ate last, the language barrier, it was a fabulous experience.

At the 1981 championship two juniors were overheard engaged in this monologue:

"Did you lose?" No response.

"Did you win?" No response.

"Did you not lose?" A shrug.

This conversation did not go anywhere, but most of the time the universal language of tennis is understood with topspin, slice, serve, volley, smash, and good shot.

16
Andre Agassi

My memory does not tell me exactly how old he was when I first met him but he must have been twelve or thirteen. It was during the early days of the Rolex International Junior Championships, and they were first staged in 1977. Our meeting and "experience" came about this way.

A few days before the tournament was to commence, I received a phone call.

"Mr. Aitchison, my name is Agassi and I want to get my son into your tournament." I replied, "I am sorry but I cannot do that, the draws are already closed and entry is only by being part of a team nominated by their country or through the qualifying rounds."

He said, "You don't understand, my son is going to be world champion one day and deserves to be in the tournament."

I countered, "I appreciate your enthusiasm, but the rules of the tournament are governed by the International Tennis Federation and I have to abide by them; the only way he can get in is if someone withdraws from the main draw at the last minute, and he is here to take that spot. I assume that he wants to play in the 14 and under division." With much frustration, he told me again how good this kid was and he would play in the 18 and under draw.

After much debate, he agreed to send his son in the

hope that he could get in. He called me back the following day with his travel arrangements and at that time I was able to tell him that a spot had opened up and that Andre had been placed in the draw.

As was the case with all visiting players, he was picked up at the airport and transported to the hotel where all the competitors were accommodated. It was here, in reception, that I met him for the first time.

I gave him an information packet that explained everything about the tournament and advised him, "Andre, you have a match at 9:15 tomorrow morning and you must not be late. If you are more than 15 minutes late after your match time, the rules tell me that I must default you. A bus will leave the hotel from the front door at 8:30 A.M. to take you to the club where the tournament is being played. You must be on that bus as the next one will not get you there in time for your match. In your packet you will find a boarding pass that will guarantee you a seat. Do you understand?" He told me that he did and we got him to his room. It was then about 10 P.M.

The next morning the 8:30 A.M. bus from the hotel arrived at the club shortly before 9:00 A.M., but Andre did not check in. Broadcasts over the P.A. system failed to locate him. I got straight on the phone to the hotel and asked for his room. He answered. I said, "Andre, why are you in your room? You are supposed to be at the club for a 9:15 match!"

His reply floored me. He calmly said, "I am waiting for the taxi you promised."

I told him, "The only taxi we provide is in the form of a bus," and I reminded him of our conversation the night before and how much I had stressed the importance of being on time. Regretfully I advised him that "the default time has arrived, and I am afraid you are out of the tournament."

I suggested that he call his father and tell him what had happened and to arrange his return travel home.

Well, about 15 minutes later we got the phone call from his dad. My wife, who was running the tournament desk, took the call and was staggered at the tirade of abuse that was coming over the line. As she had matches to put on, I think she was glad to hand the phone over to me. He ranted and raved and called me every name you can think of. It was impossible to have a conversation with him. It was so bad that I reached the stage of putting the phone down on the desk, and letting him exhaust himself. Finally, with a break in his onslaught, we got to the point of Andre returning home, and arranged to take him to the airport, where we made sure that he was on the right aircraft.

To analyze this whole situation questions need to be asked. "Was it fair to this young man to send him on his own on such a venture?" After all, he had just reached his "teens," at best; and also, "What was his father thinking?" I would not let my son travel to New York on his own, at that age. In my opinion, too much was being asked of this boy.

One thing is for sure though, Dad was right about Andre becoming a world champion one day, and what a great champion he has been.

17

S.T.A.R.T.— Sports Technique and Reaction Training

Technique and reaction training is a criterion that must be followed if you want to attain success, so when the best woman tennis player in the world, an extraordinary athlete constantly looking for a competitive edge, starts working with a bold new training system, it is intriguing enough. But when the best male tennis player in the world discovers the same system at the same time, and he too swears by its powers, it's enough to make you sit up and take notice.

That is just what happened back in 1987 when Martina Navratilova and Ivan Lendl told the sports world about START, the revolutionary fitness system that was created to help develop super champions. Martina stated then: "I have been using the START system for years and its ability to give me a well rounded conditioning and training program has been a factor in my dominance of women's tennis. There is no doubt now that the Champion's performance level will have to extend into the Super Champion status and START and I will meet this challenge together." They sure did.

Ivan was no less enthusiastic, and like Martina he was a regular user of the system. He said, "I have bettered my reaction time by 27 percent and my strength by 10 percent since starting the program. The great thing about the system is that once I have reached a certain level of proficiency I can re-program the computer so that it gives me a greater challenge." He also commented, "START also develops your reaction and movement time to such a degree that the confidence in your ability to achieve higher performance levels gives you a major competitive advantage."

This extraordinary product was developed by Rick Elstein, a U.S. tennis professional and Larry Mayol, former head trainer of the New York Mets baseball team. Because of my background in Australian tennis, I was invited to join the team being that a lot of the moves to be programmed into the computer were based on shadow drill technique, a technique used in training Australian Davis Cup players, by team coach Harry Hopman. It was my privilege to become President of the tennis division, and work with these two pros. in designing programs that would enable coaches and trainers to work on individual weaknesses, in both fitness and skill development. In my opinion, at that time, no instructional and conditioning system had been able to do so many things for every level of athletic performance, except START.

The introduction of this teaching tool into the competitive training arena marked a new era in sophisticated but simple to use equipment that simulated game situations through programmed drills. It was the only system that covered all of the parameters of training strength, flexibility, reaction and movement time, stroking techniques, shot performance, recovery and repositioning, and it was totally portable for use on and off the court. Many of the world's best tennis teaching professionals including Nick Bollettieri, Peter Burwash and Dennis Van der Meer along with numerous accredited camps, academies and individuals, incorporated it into their teaching philosophy. A particular experience for me was showing it at the French Open, Wimbledon and the U.S. Open to players from around the world. It did cause a stir at the French championships, where security wanted to check it out every day, but after a few days they recognized me as the man with the box and let me go by after I had shown them what it did.

It is described as a portable micro-processor that activates light patterns representing various moves of the game. The user makes the same move that would be made in an actual game, serve, return of serve, groundstroke, volley, overhead, etc., and does it in a pre-set time parameter, simulating hitting the ball before an audible beep tone. This is called the Beat-the-Beep challenge. Starting at a level that you can cope with, one simply modifies the time parameters to create another challenge as your ability to perform at a higher level increases. All that is required for success is the desire to raise your level of proficiency. Its use is only limited by the imagination of its user.

I still use my original machine today; however, I have never been able to master the Beat-the-Beep Challenge. It just goes on and on and on and—

18

The United States Tennis Association

My first involvement with the United States Tennis Association was in 1972 not long after my arrival in the U.S., when I took up my position with the Port Washington Tennis Academy. The P.W.T.A., which was the first of the major junior player development programs, had as part of its activities, tennis tournaments that provided for its students the opportunity to expand their skills in competitive play. As a natural follow-through, tournaments that counted for ranking on a sectional or national level were important to the players who were ambitious enough to raise their playing potential to achieve success on the sectional, national and international arenas. Part of my job was to enhance these programs so it was important that I get involved with the administration on all three levels, so as to help players achieve their goals.

For me it was to become tennis excitement plus!!! After just a few months in the United States, here I was involved in helping to develop juniors who might some day play against players from my own country that were filtering through some of the Australian programs that I had managed. In those days rivalry between these two great tennis nations was at its peak, as they both fought for world tennis supremacy, and to have sat on both sides of the fence was indeed unique.

Having an established junior tournament structure in the U.S. it was now time to provide stepping stones to the higher levels. In 1972 the Wilson Sporting Goods Company was supporting the U.S.T.A. Satellite Circuit, as it was known then, in the amount of $1200 each event for a circuit stop of six tournaments. These events catered primarily to leading amateur and college players and were the forerunners of the circuits of today, that provide such great opportunities for advancement to those seeking a career in the game. My involvement with the U.S.T.A. at that time was as co-chairman of that circuit, which would run until 1974.

During the early part of that same year, by chance I would meet the then president of American Express, Maurice Siegal, who was my next door neighbor, and an avid tennis player. He was having difficulty one Saturday morning getting his car started that would take him to his regular weekend game. I was able to help him with his problem and at the same time learn a little about his professional, social and tennis careers. As I was always looking for potential sponsors, I saw an opportunity here.

It was not long before we got to play and discuss my desire to upgrade the Satellite Circuit. His response was positive and in 1975 the American Express Circuit was born with a series of eight tournaments leading up to the U.S. Open in late August. It was my great fortune to become the administrator of this wonderful series. Each event would feature a $15,000 prize money structure and for the first time a lower level circuit would receive Association of Tennis Professional points that would help players reach the next level of competition. In 1976 a further five tournaments were added in the Western part of the country following the U.S. Open. This group of tournaments was placed on the calendar so as to accommodate players who wanted to go on to the South American, Australian and Asian circuits.

The American Express circuit flourished until 1978 when the powers that be in the U.S.T.A. decided that they wanted more control of both play and finances. Their demands on American Express were too excessive and as such, a great sponsor was lost. It was not enough to leave a good thing alone. Unfortunately, this was not to be the last of inefficient bungling that I would encounter by the administration of the so-called leading tennis nation.

During this same time, commencing in 1975, I was also involved in the U.S. Open qualifying rounds, and in fact ran the actual rounds at the Port Washington Tennis Academy. This continued until 1980, and working with the great Billy Talbert, the tournament director of the U.S. Open, was exciting and an experience in providing the world's future leading players a fighting chance to join the elite in the main draw.

I do not know what went wrong, but I assume politics reared its ugly head again and the decision was made to move the qualifying rounds elsewhere from 1981 on, until eventually they were moved to the open site, which is where they should be.

The years of 1979, 1981, 1982 and 1983 gave me the opportunity to be a U.S.T.A. administrator and tournament director with Nancy Arnaout, one of that organization's true staff members who was in charge of national junior development, and play at the then U.S. Olympic Committee's National Sports Festivals. These festivals were held in the three years when there were no summer Olympic Games, and brought together thousands of U.S. athletes representing thirty-seven sports in what could be called an American only Olympic Games. Tennis was a part of these activities and provided an opportunity for the nation's top juniors to compete in an Olympic style atmosphere. It was a privilege to meet and compete side by side with these wonderful athletes from all sports. As the political moves were being made to have tennis re-instated into the Olympic Games, these meets were imperative, and provided training and experience on how to compete under yet another type of competition. Every event was a spectacular experience.

It would eventuate that I would become the tournament director of the 1984 U.S.T.A. Olympic Tennis trials that would select United States players to compete in tennis as a demonstration sport, in the 1984 Olympic Games. Now that the sport is a permanent fixture of the summer games, the selection process is different, in that each nation selects their players based on international rankings and availability. In 1984 in the U.S., it was every player's right, through the equal opportunity act, to be given a chance to compete, hence the qualifying process, but as we all know, the best do not always come through with this method, and since status and money have ruined almost every amateur sport, it appears that we in the U.S. simply will not settle for anything less than the best. It would be nice if some of the top players, who earn millions of dollars from our sport, could put aside their need or is it greed for more, and represent their country.

I have often wondered what happened to the constitutional right for equal opportunity. I guess it went down the drain when money started to talk. Or was it pushed aside when the bastardization of the Olympics took place in the 1984 games in Los Angeles? Was that the year that the Games were up for sale? It certainly looked like it to me. Professionalism has taken over, and now every venue tries to outdo their predecessors with bigger sponsorships and more elaborate venues for events and we have joined the realms of high paid entertainment.

As the Eastern Tennis Association delegate to the

United States Tennis Association I was elected/appointed (I never will know which) to the illustrious U.S.T.A. Executive Committee in 1984–85. I was thrilled to think that I would be part of the decision-making body that would guide the U.S.T.A. through the future tennis objectives of the organization. What a joke! I soon found out that all but insignificant matters were dealt with by the "Board," that part of the Executive Committee that is elected, as opposed to the seventeen sectional delegates. I do not expect that the policy is any different today, unless those sectional delegates who sit listening to what has already been decided, really believe that they have made a contribution. However, it looks damned good on your resume to be listed on the decision-making committee of the world's most powerful tennis body. Some prospective employers may even think you are important when they see it.

The U.S.T.A. Junior Tennis Council chairmanship came to me in 1985–86. At that time this council played a major role in developing the sport throughout the country, and was foremost in conducting national junior circuits through member clubs. The council was responsible for all policies relating to junior training and competition and worked closely with the sections to implement those policies. As a member of the council since 1974, I was seeing the changes that the game was making and the important role that juniors would play as they grew into this new era. There were plenty of bumps along the way, many created by our own Executive Officers, some of whom were quick to move the blame if anything went wrong.

It was very evident that the game's best players were going to be younger in the future, and that training methods would change. A number of training camps were held throughout the country, using the best coaches including Nick Bollettieri and Dennis Van der Meer, and our top juniors were exposed to intensive drilling, fitness and playing programs. It had to be understood, that to compete on a world class level you had to be a world class athlete, and these training camps were the stepping stones to the eventual player development program. The culmination of this thinking would show in the U.S. Open Junior Championships. Here, players would come from all parts of the world to compete in one of the grand slams of junior tennis, and the talent that would be displayed confirmed the practicality of our training camps. As a member of the U.S. Open Junior Championship Committee at that time, it was extremely pleasing to see the outstanding tennis that these players produced. Today we can admire the performance of these young athletes who are now competing at the open international level.

At the U.S. Open in 1984, the then president elect of the U.S.T.A., Randy Gregson, said to me, "Aitchison, do we need a player development program?"

My reply was simple and to the point due to the work that the junior tennis council was doing. "You bet we do, what has taken us so long? Australia, Canada, Germany and Sweden all have established programs and we are dragging our feet."

He replied, "Good, I think that too, and I want you to be a full-time consultant to me and the board to get it started."

I was dazed by his proposal, and mentioned that I already had a full-time job to which he said, "Let's change all that."

With the ever-growing tension of administering the Port Washington Tennis Academy due to the terminal illness of Hy Zausner and the return of his "prodigal" son, my resignation was imminent. I made the decision and in May of 1985, with Gregson now the President of the U.S.T.A., and the "Board" approving, I got started on the program.

My initial task was to find an appropriate location from a weather perspective, as the importance of all-year-round training in an outdoor environment was essential. The vast majority of major tournaments are conducted outdoors on various surfaces and the climatic conditions often govern the outcome of a match. We needed a climate that would allow us to provide those conditions on a multi-surface basis. My travels took me to many parts of the country but it soon became clear that to fit our policy it would be necessary to have our facility in either the West or South of the country. Cities such as Indianapolis, where I was honored with a presentation of a key to the city (no, it was not a bribe), Salt Lake City, Jacksonville, Fla., San Diego and Bradenton were among the forefront of the venues to be considered. The Bradenton site, which was the Bollettieri Tennis Academy, seemed the perfect selection, having different court surfaces, a gymnasium, video replay and recreation facilities, among other things, plus accommodations. Here was a place that was already built and up and running which would take the chore out of starting from scratch. It was also for sale. It was so impressive that the U.S.T.A. put down a deposit pending further negotiations. Unfortunately it was not to be and the sale did not come to fruition. Not long after, the facility was bought by the International Management Group who today runs it as a multi-sport training academy (including tennis) for both students and coaches.

In a *Tennis Week* interview on October 3rd, 1985 President Randy Gregson stated, "Our big problem is that we are not getting the best athletes, so we will create a national training center that will house and train a crop of America's most promising junior players. Aitchison, who is the chairman of the national junior tennis council, will head up the training center once it is established."

Unfortunately this never happened once the political

wheels started to turn. I have it on good authority that some powers did not want an Australian heading up this national program. It was a bitter disappointment for me given my proven credentials, my years of work with juniors on the national level, and my desire to bring the cream to the top, whatever the nationality. However, it was a dual experience, positive in the creation of the idea and the initial planning that brought about the program of today, but negative in the weakness of the upper echelon not to back me in its implementation.

During my twenty-six years of volunteer service (1972–98) to the United States Tennis Association, I served on many committees and spent countless hours doing what I loved to do, serve tennis and its participants. All of these I cherish and will have enough memories to reflect on for the rest of my life. It is impossible to put everything into words, but if you can journey with me down memory lane using your own imagination, you will perhaps get an idea of my involvement in this great game. Here is the listing: Co-chairman, U.S.T.A. Satellite Circuit 1972–74; Administrator, American Express Circuit 1975–78; Member U.S. Open Qualifying Rounds Committee and Tournament Director 1975–80; Member U.S.T.A. Junior Tennis Council 1974–86; Chairman U.S.T.A. Junior Tennis Council 1985–86; U.S.T.A. Administrator and Tournament Director for Tennis at the U.S. Olympic Committee National Sports Festivals 1979–81, 82–83; Guest speaker U.S.T.A. National Teachers Conferences 1980–82, 83; Tournament Director U.S.T.A. Olympic Tennis Trials 1984; Member U.S.T.A. Executive Committee 1984–85; guest speaker International Tennis Federation World Wide Tennis Teachers Conference 1986; Former Chairman U.S.T.A. Amateur Championships and Girls 12–14–16 National Indoor Championships; Former member of the U.S.T.A. Circuit Regulations Committee,

U.S. Open Junior Championships committee, U.S.T.A. Olympic Committee, U.S.T.A. Junior Davis Cup Committee and the Technical Committee.

Presidents of the United States Tennis Association are the executive officers and are also chairmen of the U.S. Open Tennis Championships. A monumental task and one that takes much dedication to the sport. Their backgrounds, walks of life, talents and visions are all different except for one thing. It seems to me that each of them needs to leave a monument or legacy that belongs only to them. In my years, I could never see a clear-cut, long range plan that followed through to the next leader without it being modified to suit the sitting president. Perhaps the exception to this was, (a) the building of the national tennis center in Flushing Meadows Park, New York where "Slew" Hester, president 1977–78, was credited with fulfilling this massive task, and honored for his work with a plaque depicting his efforts, which, incidentally, is proudly displayed at the facility. I know personally of the sacrifice he made in carrying out this achievement, as I was part of the background force that worked around the clock for the opening of the new stadium in 1978. (b) The renovation of that same center with President Harry Marmion (1997–98) at the helm. There is no doubt that planning had been going on for some years by many people to upgrade the center to world class standards, and rightly so. A magnificent job was done with the reconfiguration of the grounds and outside courts, making it easy for patrons to view the many fine matches that are played away from the main stadiums, in the early rounds of the tournament. Even the reduction in seating size of the original Louis Armstrong Stadium was a good move, in that the new Arthur Ashe Stadium was the centerpiece of the renovation.

The Ashe Stadium concept was exciting architecturally

with greatly improved amenities, but in this writer's opinion, badly flawed by its twenty-three thousand odd seating capacity. Tennis is supposed to be an intimate sport where players and fans can interact, and this cannot happen if your only choice of seats is in the "nose bleed" sections, and these are often the only seats available to the general public.

I have had many patrons tell me, you cannot see the ball or hear it struck and cannot even recognize the players. This is not the way to promote our game and it certainly is not right to charge ridiculously high prices, just for the satisfaction of being there. You have to wonder who made this outlandish decision, or was it because we in America have an overwhelming desire to be the biggest and the best, at all costs? (c) The USA Tennis Plan for Growth program is a commitment that the U.S.T.A. should have, and is one that through its various stages such as Tennis America and USA Tennis 123, has brought many new players into the game, and has been highly successful. These programs, designed as introductory basic learning of tennis skills, have passed through different administrations and were put squarely on the map in the last two years of the last century.

The question is, why are these programs not titled, U.S.T.A.? Why have we taken on the role of being the "Country?" We are simply *part of it*. It seems to me that we have forsaken the identity of our own organization, which is indeed national, but is not yet understood by players who are still outside the stream of tournament and league play.

All in all, we stagger along much like the lumbering dinosaurs of yesteryear: small head with limited far-reaching brain power (the executive committee), a huge body (the sections and their volunteers, who really make the game move), and a thrashing tail (the tennis-playing public who get pushed in all directions through lack of information and uncertain decisions on policy, programs and events).

Perhaps one day the U.S.T.A. will find a leader who can bring all parts of the beast together so that we may see growth in our Sport of a Lifetime. Surely it is time for the Executive Committee to model itself along the lines of any successful corporation, and charge the professional staff and the sections to carry out the policies that make for growth. I hope I live to see it.

The following are the presidents who held office during my service to the U.S.T.A. and my one line impressions of them. No offense intended, it's just the way I saw you all.

1973–74	Walter E. Elcock	Sincere leader looking to lead.
1975–76	Stanley Malless	You never knew if he was with you or against you.
1977–78	W.E. (Slew) Hester	Tough, honest and got the job done.
1979–80	Joseph E. Carrico	A facts and figures disciplinarian.
1981–82	Marvin P. Richmond	Reminded me of the movie *The Great Dictator*.
1983–84	Hunter L. Delatour, Jr.	By far the most appealing and sincere.
1985–86	J. Randolph Gregson	Lots of promises but did not carry through with them.
1987–88	Gordon D. Jorgensen	Mr. Who's Who in engineering, industry and finance in the world—but tennis?
1989–90	David R. Markin	Successful, tough negotiator and a decision maker.

1991–92	Robert A. Cookson	Nice guy but a shadow of his predecessor.
1993–94	J. Howard (Bumpy) Frazer	A smart man who could not make up his mind.
1995–96	Lester M. Snyder, Jr.	Should have had a legacy but was in the wrong place at the wrong time.
1997–98	Harry A. Marmion	Much like the Washington politicians.

It would be most unfair not to mention the history-making entry of the first woman president even though it is outside of my service years. By the time this book is in print, she will have made her mark in the so-called "scheme of things" one way or another, and there will be those with better skills than I, to document her efforts.

1999–2000	Julia A. Levering	The first woman president of the U.S.T.A. Smiles at everything, and why not, she was the first female to run the show.

P.S. At the time of writing in 2005, one such president had just completed his term and seemed to have put things in their right perspective. A professional in creating innovative tennis programs and a leader in the tennis world, Alan G. Schwartz took our game to new heights with his knowledge and ability to lead us into the future. It is hoped that his successors will continue with his passion to grow the game.

Billie Jean King—1962. Photo courtesy of World Team Tennis.

Margaret Court in action.

Chris Evert Lloyd—Orange Bowl Champion 1969, 1970, seeded #2, 1986 U.S. Open Singles. Photo courtesy of Russ Adams Productions, Inc.

Wimbledon Champion Evonne Goolagong receiving a copper bracelet from admirer Joanne Tridcey, 1971. Photo courtesy of the Australian News and Information Bureau.

Geoff Masters, Patrice Dominguez, Collin Dibbley, and Patrick Proisy during a rain break at the Australian Open tennis championships, 1971. Photo courtesy of the Australian News and Information Bureau.

Ivan Lendl—Orange Bowl Champion, 1977, seeded #1, 1986 U.S. Open Singles. Photo courtesy of Russ Adams Productions, Inc.

Rod Laver in action.

The stylish Ken Rosewall in action.

Peter Fleming, UCLA

Kathleen Horvath and Jimmy Arias as juniors with Roland Puton (of Rolex) and Alex. Aitchison. Photo courtesy of Russ Adams Productions, Inc.

Alex. (center) and Marjorie (seated) Aitchison celebrate a Davis Cup victory with some friends at the United States Tennis Association's annual meeting, 1983.

Virginia Wade (center) with Alex. and Marjorie Aitchison, 1997.

Some fatherly advice on the next point, Moscow, USSR, 1989. Photo courtesy of the Remington Archives.

Alex. Aitchison (right) presenting Sam Shore with a Hall of Fame sculpture, 1992.

Alex. Aitchison—Eastern Tennis Association Man of the Year, 1992. Photo courtesy of Sam Berman.

Eastern Tennis Family of the Year. Left to right: Grant, Scott, Marjorie, Alex., and Perry.

Exhibition play with Vijay Armitraj.

Inductees to the Eastern Tennis Hall of Fame, 2002. Left to right: Bob Ryland, Alex. Aitchison, Kathy Horvath, and Paul Annacone. Photo courtesy of Ed Goldman.

Alex. Aitchison with wife, Marjorie (left) and presenter, Barbara Williams (right), at his induction into the Eastern Tennis Hall of Fame.

19

In Quest of Excellence

As a tennis consultant and teaching professional, I was often amazed that some proficient players showed little desire to take their games to the next level. I believe that the prime object of playing this great sport is to have fun, but those who have aspirations of achieving success in competitive play, must go further in trying to reach their goals.

In an attempt to bring out the significance of this important phase of the game, I was inspired to write the following 12 disciplines for better tennis that, if followed, will certainly lead to excellence. Becoming a better tennis player is more than just hitting balls over the net and hoping that your opponent will make mistakes. You must master every facet of the game and challenge yourself to meet goals. Even the best players in the world have to constantly challenge themselves to achieve greater heights. Whatever your level, following these disciplines will improve your game if you understand and practice them.

Fitness

Tennis legend Harry Hopman, who during the '50s and '60s captained the Australian Davis Cup teams and brought his players to victory 15 out of 19 times, believed that if all things were equal, fitness is the one quality that will win a match. Fitness means physical and mental preparation. Physical fitness requires a well-designed program to increase your cardio-vascular output, develop your muscle complex, and improve endurance.

Many professional programs are available to suit your goals for your level of participation. Former world class player, Jim Courier, had a unique approach by running with car tires tied to his waist. Others run up and down sand dunes on the beach.

Mental fitness should also be a major part of your regime. Being alert with a clear mind, not befuddled by drugs, smoking or unnecessary medications, will enhance your performance. A top professional will reveal the level of their mental fitness in their eyes.

Stamina

Stamina is resistance to fatigue. Standout players like Pete Sampras, Patrick Rafter, Andre Agassi, Martina Navratilova, Steffi Graf and the Williams sisters, could stay in the point for long periods of time without becoming fatigued, contributing to their success. They had learned that in the final set, stamina and endurance counted.

To achieve this discipline, study the average number of strokes you require to win a point. For example, if it takes you five strokes to win a baseline rally, four for side-to-side baseline running, three volleys and two overhead smashes, multiply each by five and practice hitting them all in one drill. Have a friend or your teaching professional hit the balls to you so that you are continually hitting, running and stretching.

You must also learn to breathe properly. Here is a good

breathing drill. Inhale through your nose on the way to the ball (your nose has filters to clean the air as it enters your lungs), exhale through your mouth as you strike the ball, inhale on your recovery, exhale at recovery, and repeat for as many shots as necessary to win the point. After each point or exercise drill take three or four deep breaths using this formula, holding the air in your lungs for three or four seconds before exhaling. When you can do the drill without feeling fatigue you have the stamina necessary for that stroke. To build up and maintain your stamina throughout a match, combine baseline running, rallies, volleys and overhead smashes into 16 or 20 ball drills and repeat four times.

Flexibility

Stretching exercises are the most important way to improve your flexibility, although they are overlooked in many training programs. You need to warm up and cool down every part of your body from your neck to your toes, before and after play. If not, you may strain a ligament or tendon or tear a muscle, all debilitating injuries that affect your performance. Practice singles drills on the doubles court and stretch for every ball even if you know you cannot reach it. This will enhance your ability to reach balls you thought were impossible to get in match play. If you can get your racquet on or close to balls in the doubles court, you should be able to reach almost everything in the singles court.

Reaction

Imagine jumping to safety to avoid a falling facade off a

building as you walk along a pavement, or dodging a vehicle speeding toward you as you cross a street. This is reaction. In tennis, you react to a ball hit by your opponent. Reaction is built into all of us; however, some react more quickly than others. This is a discipline that we all need to work on so as to improve our performance level. To improve reaction time, on-court volley drills are best because a volley exchange at the net generates the quickest movement you have to make to return the ball. Have your teaching pro or friend, feed balls to you quickly, or practice "shadow drills" in which you have to change direction after you have committed to go another way.

There are various machines on the market that require you to move your body, feet and hands in a given direction, selected by randomly flashing lights. Exacting discipline is a must requirement to better your reaction time, and the more quickly you react will translate to greater body speed.

Speed

Not to be confused with reaction, is rapid motion, swiftness, velocity, or rate of movement. In tennis, it is measuring the shortest period of time required to get to the ball. Speed, in getting from point A, where you are, to point B, where the ball is, is essential to good shot selection and stroke production. Forward dashes (to get to drop shots) or baseline dashes (to get to down the line drives), which are timed by a stopwatch or a machine designed to measure the time it takes to cover distance, are invaluable speed improvement drills. You must challenge yourself to move more quickly to the ball each time you walk on the court.

Focus

Tennis requires both visual and mental focus. Visual focus means tracking the ball with your eyes as it moves back and forth between you and your opponent during a point. It tells your brain that you want to approach the ball so that you can hit it and return it to your opponent's side of the net. Eye contact with the ball creates a communication process which generates motivation of the body necessary to strike the ball. You must maintain eye contact with the ball for the full duration of the point, to complete a successful rally.

Mental focus comes into play when you return the ball. It is that innate desire to hit a shot so well it is un-returnable. To do this, you need mental focus to hit the ball where it will be impossible for your opponent to return. In your mind, picture where you would like the ball to go. Create a mental target on the opposite side of the court for every shot that you hit, but keep your eye focus on the ball, not on the target. Don't break the visual communication with your brain. If you learn to focus well, you are on your way to establishing excellent concentration skills.

Concentration

This discipline places all of your attention on a given shot in a point being played. Too often confused with focus, all of your concentration needs to be applied to shot selection, stroking technique, body rotation, foot placement, foot speed and balance—in effect, what are you going to do with the ball and how are you going to do it. Shot selection occurs as soon as the ball leaves your opponent's racket. First you must determine what type of ball you are receiving, whether it is topspin, slice, sidespin, flat, slow, medium, or fast, and you only have the time it takes for the ball to reach you to make this decision. Then, you must decide how to counteract this shot. Jimmy Connors made the greatest impression on me as one who had the best of concentration skills. He was literally consumed when he was playing the point, but could relax with the crowd when the point was over.

Concentration alone is not enough to win the point, however. You must be able to get to the ball, rotate and balance your body, and step into the shot correctly. Your teaching professional is your best source for this information and training.

Power

In recent years, players have developed the ability to serve the ball at 130 MPH-plus and U.S. Davis Cup player Andy Roddick actually clocked one at 154 MPH.

Combine this with dazzling 100 MPH ground strokes and you have mind-boggling exchanges. Power is the name of the game in tennis being played today.

Power is the ability to strike the ball with maximum energy. Another definition of power is physical force. These elevated power levels require you to enhance your reaction, focus, speed, flexibility and concentration. If not, you're out of the point.

The power game as displayed by the professionals, has influenced the rank and file players as they try to emulate what they see, sometimes to their detriment, not realizing that it takes dedication and hours of hard work to perfect these skills. Even juniors feel that they have to hit the ball harder than ever to achieve a result.

The problem with power is that it is useless without control.

Control

Control means hitting the ball with consistency regardless of the power used to strike the ball. Andre Agassi, Lindsay Davenport, Steffi Graf and Rod Laver go down as some of the best practitioners of control. It is that discipline that restrains you from over-hitting. If you lose control, it affects your stroking technique and changes the result of your shot. It is far better to reduce power in order to gain more control.

Restraint

Is an integral part of control because it holds your emotions in check. Losing emotional control leads to so many lost points, games, sets and matches. Making judgment errors during a point is human. No one plays the "perfect" game. Learning how to lose without becoming emotionally upset is a talent equal to that of being happy when you win. You are the only one who can restrain yourself from these "mind-breaking" episodes. Not doing so leads to anger and bad sportsmanship. To relax is the secret; take some deep breaths, shrug your shoulders, take a short walk, fiddle with the strings, or count to ten to release the tension.

Unfortunately, unsportsmanlike conduct has been in our game for generations and used by some to gain an unfair advantage over their opponents. Take John McEnroe, for example: Did he ever complain when he was winning? No, he carried on his tirades only when challenged. Was this

his way of unsettling his opponents? Ilie Nastase was rude and crude, often spitting at his opponents and stalling, so as to break their concentration. Jimmy Connors was downright indecent, sometimes touching his private parts, and on one occasion I saw him actually drop his shorts and "moon" the crowd as he was leaving the grounds, having just lost a match. No one questions their ability on the court, but surely these antics come under the heading of bad sportsmanship.

There is absolutely no excuse for players of this caliber not to be able to restrain themselves from these practices. After all, the top professionals are the role models for our up and coming juniors.

Performance

Whether you compete socially or competitively, you strive to perform at your best. Performance is the result of your efforts, and will be enhanced if you master these twelve disciplines. Perhaps the greatest mistake you can make is being forced into playing your opponent's game. When you don't play your own game you will make errors. Although the basics are the same and necessary for everyone, you have your own style and should play the game you know. Stick to the strokes that you are comfortable with and play your best. You will find this plan the most satisfying.

Satisfaction

Whatever your ability level, satisfaction comes from being the best you can be. If after you have played your best against a well matched opponent, you can walk off the court with a smile, irrespective of the score, you are truly a champion.

To begin to reach your personal potential and achieve your highest standard of performance, it is necessary to first make the commitment, then, dedicate yourself to putting forth maximum energy and full concentration in attaining your goals. You alone hold the key to your success. If you are fully committed, nothing can stop you. Whether you are at a practice session or playing a tournament match, applying the following will help. (1) Be on time and prepared to start when requested. (2) Be sure of why you are there. Know your goals and what you need to do to achieve them. (3) Concentrate all of your energy in working toward your goal. (4) Prepare fully, both physically and mentally for the activity to come. (5) Have a positive and cooperative attitude. This will enhance your performance. (6) Use your time effectively. (7) Listen carefully, look critically and move efficiently. (8) When finished, ask yourself, "Did I give it my best?"

20

The Chiquita Cup

In my endeavors to constantly promote the game of tennis, I came in contact with numerous individuals, groups and organizations that were looking to get involved in the tennis explosion. There were many opportunities for sponsorship and it became a matter of who could fit with what program, or in some cases, it meant developing an event to suit the needs of an interested party. I had been toying with the idea of an event leading up to the U.S. Open, and was contemplating the age group of twenty-one and under.

As good fortune would have it, I met a figure from an organization called "People to People Sports." This was a group that had ties to the White House in Washington, D.C. and received funding to promote good will with other nations and expand the cultural bonds through sport, on a global basis. I explained my idea and was asked to develop a program that would bring nations together at a time when tennis would be at peak interest in the tennis calendar year. I thought all of my birthdays had come at once. It was a perfect scenario.

I put pen to paper, scratched my head, and came up with a sixteen country team event for twenty-one and under players. The proposal was to play the tournament in the week leading up to the qualifying rounds of the U.S. Open. The venue would be New York's Central Park, just twenty minutes away from the National Tennis Center. A budget was developed and the total plan was submitted by the People to People group to a potential sponsor, the United Brands Company. They accepted the proposal, and agreed to cover the tournament costs through one of their holdings, Chiquita Bananas. The stage was now set for the first International Young Masters Chiquita Cup Championship to be played in the United States. The year was 1980.

The New York City Parks and Recreation department was very cooperative in working with us in staging this event, and the players who frequented this facility got behind the excitement of having an international hard-court tournament on their home courts.

Invitations were sent out to affiliated nations of the International Tennis Federation and sixteen teams comprising two men and two women each, were accepted.

The United States Tennis Association had given its blessing for the event but cautioned that because the Chiquita Cup final was on the same day as the first day of the U.S. Open qualifying rounds, some conflict might arise. However, officials assured me that every effort would be made to avoid this situation.

The competition commenced with a parade of nations before a large gallery of spectators, including our sponsors, after which the process of elimination started.

Outstanding tennis was played by all representatives of their countries during the tournament, but it seemed inevitable that two arch rivals, in Australia and the United States, would be the teams contesting for the title. On the final day, it was in fact these two teams that would battle for supremacy.

Throughout the tournament I was in constant contact with the U.S. Open qualifying rounds officials about who was still involved, and they advised me that the players competing in our final would have to register their names with the tournament committee at Flushing Meadows, as being present. As directed, the players concerned reported at 8:30 A.M. on the day in question and were told that they would not be required until the sixth round of matches, which would be at approximately 6:00 P.M. This was perfect, as our final was due to climax at around 3:00 P.M.

A sponsor luncheon was held on this day at the Tavern On The Green restaurant in Central Park, and some very influential guests were present. It was our hope that they might become participants in furthering this event through their sponsorship programs and we had perceived excellent indications throughout the event that this could happen.

During lunch I was receiving an up-date on play every fifteen minutes, and every one was anxious to get back to the match.

Not long after our guests and sponsors had settled into viewing this exciting struggle again (the U.S. was leading Australia 3 rubbers to 2 in a seven rubber match), the un-imaginable happened.

I received a message from the U.S. Open qualifying committee that the players were being called for their matches at 3:00 P.M. If they did not respond within fifteen minutes after that, they would be defaulted. The time was just after 1:00 P.M. Their matches were no longer at 6:00 P.M. as previously told earlier in the day. I appealed immediately, but was rejected. With the time now after 2:00 P.M., and the status of our match making it impossible to finish, have our presentation, and get the players to Flushing Meadows by 3:00 P.M., I had no alternative but to advise the captains of the situation. Together, they went on to the court and presented the dilemma to their teams. After a short discussion, the Americans were content to continue, but the Australians decided that they had no alternative but to concede the Chiquita Cup, and flee to Flushing Meadows in a van. It was a tough decision, but in hindsight, they had come a long way for the opportunity to get into a grand-slam event, and they needed to give it a try. It was not their fault that they had been put into this position.

As you can imagine, there was pandemonium. The "People to People Sports" group were running around and screaming at me, "You can't do this!" The sponsors were asking, "What is going on?" and I was absolutely stunned. How could this have happened?

I was now in the awkward situation of having to explain to our sponsors, their guests, my co-organizers, the other players, and the spectators, the reason for this sudden conclusion to our event. At the time, the only information that I had was what had been translated to the two captains, so with apologies, that is what I explained.

I can tell you that there was absolute rage in the sponsorship camp that a $500,000 venture had literally blown up in their faces.

On investigation, it was clear that the Chiquita Cup had been wrecked by a masterful stroke of administrative bungling by the officials of the U.S. Open qualifying rounds. At some point of time in the morning, the decision was made to reduce the size of the qualifying draw from its normal 128 competitors to 96, to "maintain the quality of a Grand Slam event," which in turn changed the playing program. No consideration was given to the earlier time schedule laid out to the players.

When the players arrived at Flushing Meadows, which took them an hour in New York's busy traffic, one American and one Australian had been defaulted by the referee and the Grand Prix supervisor, but the other Australian, who was principally responsible for the abandonment of the team event, was told, "Oh sorry, you needn't have come after all, you've gone straight into the main draw."

It was then that everyone realized that there had been no need for the sudden death of the Chiquita Cup.

The upshot that followed was anger, frustration and total lack of confidence in the U.S.T.A. and their officials in charge of the qualifying rounds, by all of us associated with presenting this new and magnificent tennis event to the tennis world. A meeting with the president of the U.S.T.A. during the following U.S. Open failed to bring even an apology for the incident, and a potential law suit by the sponsor was dropped in disgust. Needless to say, they withdrew any future financial support to tennis and the Chiquita Cup was history.

From my point of view, the concept of the event was great but the conclusion was a bitter experience. It made me wonder at the time, *Why continue?*

It was suggested that perhaps the U.S.T.A. was trying to sabotage the event, but I failed to find any reason why they should do that, being that it had their blessing. Personally, I am convinced to this day, that the U.S. Open qualifying officials were intent on running their own show, and any other event that might conflict with their program should be put on a back burner. No thought was given to the long range plan for more sponsorship and new events.

Fortunately, life goes on as we strive to do better, in spite of the obstacles—and we continue to reach and achieve higher goals.

21

People

People, it is often said, are the one element that makes the world go around. Certainly our interaction with each other contributes largely to our learning and behavior patterns and helps in the decision-making process for the next steps that we take in life.

We are influenced by the actions of others and those we admire for their skills and articulate ways. and these are often emulated in our own style and character. In my lifetime of tennis I have been blessed with an abundance of people in that sport from whom I could draw the ideas and energy necessary to complete, for me, a successful career. As I look back, my relationship with these human beings was like the growth of a tree. The sap getting its strength from the roots and then bursting forth into a strong forceful presence, with strong limbs and branches reaching outward to the world.

Many thousands of tennis players, administrators and officials played a major part in my life, most at the grass roots level of learning, playing their first tournaments, rising through the different levels of competition, and being satisfied that they had reached their own personal ability level, and played at that level with the same fervor as the top players.

It has been my privilege that over the six decades I have been involved in the game, I have made contact with some of the greats, either through play, tournament directorship, or just plain friendship. The following is a partial list of those wonderful players of whom I am proud to say, "I knew you." Some, just touching like a breath of wind as they went by, others for longer and more frequent experiences, and those who have remained with me through this long journey. I beg your indulgence for this trip down memory lane.

Terry Addison, Andre Agassi, Ronald Agenor, John Alexander, Aktar Ali, Leslie Allen, Victor Amaya, Vijay Amritraj, Mal Anderson, Jorge Andrew, Paul Annacone, Patricio Aprey, Jimmy Arias, Laura Arraya, Arthur Ashe, John Austin, Tracy Austin, Ian Ayre.

Syd Ball, Corrado Barazzutti, John Barrett, Pierre Barthes, Carling Bassett, Jeremy Bates, Lindsey Beaven, Boris Becker, John Beddington, Ramiro Benevides, Paola Bertolucci, Byron Black, James Blake, Nancye Bolton, Bjorn Borg, Bill Bowrey, Norman Brookes, John Bromwich, John Brown, Earl "Butch" Buchholz, Maria Bueno, Curt Buesman, Bettina Bunge, Wilheim Bungert, Elise Burgin, Peter Burwash.

Mike Cahill, Francesco Cancellotti, Paolo Cane, Don Candy, Jennifer Capriati, Kent Carlssen, Mary Carillo, Bob Carmichael, Rosie Casals, Ross Case, Pat Cash, Lesley Charles, Jimmy Connors, Ashley Cooper, John Cooper, Patricio Cornejo, Margaret Court, Mark Cox, Patrick Cramer, Paul Cranis, Dick Crealy, Ian Crookenden, Kevin Curren.

Judy Dalton, Sarah Palfrey Danzig, Pierre Darmon, Lindsay Davenport, Owen Davidson, Scott Davis, Donald Dell, Phil Dent, Steve Denton, Diane Desfor, Eddie Dibbs, Colin Dibley, Peter Doerner, Colin Dowdeswell, Roger Dowdeswell, Jaraslav Drobny, Cliff Drysdale, Pat Dupre, Francois Durr.

Robyn Ebbern, Stefan Edberg, Mark Edmondson, Peter Elter, Jacco Eltingh, Roy Emerson, Tomas Enquist, Mike Estep, Chris Evert.

Rosalyn Fairbank, Bob Falkenberg, Trevor Fancutt, Trish Faulkner, John Feaver, Mary Jo Fernandez, Wayne Ferreira, Jamie Fillol, Peter Fleming, Ian Fletcher, Ken Fletcher, Don Fontana, Allen Fox, Neale Fraser, Rod Frawley, Amy Frazier, Richard Fromberg, Dianne Fromholtz, Eric Fromm, Shirley Fry, Bettina Fulco.

Alvin Gardiner, Zina Garrison, Ruta Gerulaitis, Vitas Gerulaitis, Sam Giammalva, Althea Gibson, Brad Gilbert, Dana Gilbert, Wendy Gilchrist, Hans Gildemeister, Laura Gildemeister, Bob Giltinan, Andres Gimeno, Juan Gisbert, Raquel Giscafre, Shlomo Glickstein, Andres Gomez, Francisco Gonzalez, Pancho Gonzalez, Evonne Goolagong, Tom Gorman, Brian Gottfried, Larry Gottfried, Helen Gourlay, Georges Goven, Carol Graebner, Tim Gullikson, Tom Gullikson, Heinz Gunthardt, Michele Gurdal.

Barbara Hallquist, Charles Hare, Mary Hare, Rex Hartwig, Otto Hauser, Gladys Heldman, Julie Heldman, Bob Hewitt, Lew Hoad, Ron Holmberg, Harry Hopman, Nell Hopman, Kathleen Horvath, Humphrey Hose, Bob Howe, Petra Huber, Paul Hutchins, Patricia Hy.

Goran Ivanisevic.

Warren Jacques, Andrea Jaeger, Susy Jaeger, John James, Andres Jarryd, Luke Jensen, Murphy Jensen, Shirley Jones, Kathy Jordan, Boro Jovanovic.

Kathy Keil, Doug Kelso, Damir Keretic, Billie Jean King, Carlos Kirmayr, Jack Kramer, Karen Krantzke, Johan Kreik, Aaron Krickstein, Ramanathan Krishnan, Paul Kronk, Steve Krulevitz, Christian Kuhnke, Jan Kukal.

Premjit Lall, Jay Lapidus, Marcelo Lara, Rod Laver, Andrea Leand, Jan Lehane, Ivan Lendl, Susan Leo, Chris Lewis, Richard Lewis, Elizabeth Little, David Lloyd, John

Lloyd, Colin Long, Thelma Long, Maureen "Peanut" Louie, Bob Lutz.

Doug MacCurdy, Barry Mackay, Lorne Main, Hana Mandlikova, Amos Mansdorf, Bruce Manson, Bob Mark, John Marks, Billy Martin, Susan Mascarin, Geoff Masters, Helga Masthoff, Wally Masur, Stanley Matthews, Alex Mayer, Gene Mayer, Sandy Mayer, Tim Mayotte, John McEnroe, Patrick McEnroe, Ian McGregor, Chuck McKinley, Jim McManus, Frew McMillan, Peter McNamara, Paul McNamee, Kerry Melville, Sashi Menon, Alex Metreveli, Glen Michibata, Anne Minter, Bernie Mitton, Claudia Monteiro, Penny Moor, Ray Moore, Gussie Moran, Olga Morozova, Jaidip Mukerjea, Martin Mulligan, Gardnar Mulloy, Jennifer Mundel, Thomas Muster.

Betsy Nagelsen, Ilie Nastase, Jana Novotna, Martina Navratilova, Janet Newberry, John Newcombe, Yannick Noah, Juan Nunez, Bhannu Nunna, Joakim Nystrom.

Tom Okker, Alex Olmedo, Christine O'Neil, Manuel Orantes, Rafael Osuna, Wendy Overton.

Dinny Pails, John Paish, Tony Palafox, Jared Palmer, Adriano Panatta, Pascale Paradis, Onny Parun, Charlie Pasarell, Mercedes Paz, Fred Perry, Eva Pfaff, Terry Phelps, Tony Pickard, Nicola Pietrangeli, Nikki Pilic, Barbara Potter, John Powless, Maureen Pratt, Patrick Proisy.

Adrian Quist.

Beverly Rae, Patrick Rafter, Dennis Ralston, Raul Ramirez, Jouquim Rascado, Richard Raskin, Kerry Reid, Wayne Reid, Richey Reneberg, Peter Rennert, Sandra Reynolds, Renee Richards, Cliff Richey, Nancy Richey, Marty Riessen, Bobby Riggs, Lorraine Robinson, Tony Roche, Mervyn Rose, Ken Rosewall, Kym Ruddell, Ray Ruffles, Jo Anne Russell, Richard Russell.

Sue Saliba, Lennart Sandstrom, Mike Sangster, Manuel Santana, Dick Savitt, Bill Scanlon, Ted Schroeder, Gene

Scott, Frank Sedgman, Abe Segal, Pancho Segura, Vic Seixas, Russell Seymour, Winnie Shaw, Sam Shore, Pam Shriver, Billy Sidwell, Jeff Simpson, Russell Simpson, Orlando Sirola, Anne Smith, Paula Smith, Stan Smith, Peter Smylie, Joao Soares, Harold Solomon, Jennifer Staley, Sherwood Stewart, Graham Stilwell, Dick Stockton, Fred Stolle, Allan Stone, Betty Stove, Hana Strachonova, Eric Sturgess.

Sergio Tacchini, Bill Talbert, Roscoe Tanner, Catherine Tanvier, Ferdi Taygan, Roger Taylor, Brian Teacher, Pam Teeguarden, Eliot Teltscher, Andrea Temesvari, Rolf Thung, Ion Tiriac, Wendy Turnbull, Leslie Turner, Tony Trabert.

Torben Ulrich.

Erik Van Dillen, King Van Nostrand, Vince Van Patten, Robert Van't Hof, Yvonne Vermaak, Guillermo Vilas.

Virginia Wade, Sharon Walsh, Butch Walts, Trey Waltke, Kim Warwick, Malivai Washington, Marianne Werdel, Michael Westphal, Anne White, Pam Whytcross, Mats Wilander, Tim Wilkison, Owen Williams, Sidney Wood, Warren Woodcock, Martin Wostenholme.

Ricardo Ycaza, Dulcy Young.

Vladimir Zednik.

There are many more uncountable numbers of people not listed here that made up my tennis life, and in many ways they were the main ingredients of the small part I played in the game.

I have valued the friendship of those who were by my side in various projects and added to my own expertise through their knowledge that they shared with me. Isn't it true that almost everything we know has been learnt from someone else?

Here are some of those "teachers" whose patience and guidance served me well.

Administration:

Rolla Anderson, David Benjamin, Ray Benton, Francesco Ricci-Bitti, Jane Brown, Gene Buwick, Ian Carson, Philippe Chartrier, John Coman, Joseph Cullman, Jim Entink, Ed Fernberger, Marilyn Fernberger, Les Fitz Gibbon, Tony Gathercole, Eve Kraft, Peter Lawler, Alastair Martin, Jack May, Mark McCormack, Jim McManus, Ella Musolino, Nick Powell, Marty Rotberg, Larry Scott, Alphonso Smith, Ted Sperry, Cliff Sproule, Brian Tobin, Alan Urban, James Van Alen, Barbara Wancke, Henry Wancke, James Westhall, Roy Wilder, Owen Williams, Shirley Woodhead, Barbara Wynne, John Young.

Coaches:

George Bacso, Brian Barker, Nick Bollettieri, Derek Bone, Bob Brett, Peter Burwash, Darren Cahill, Vic Edwards, Rick Elstein, John Fitzgerald, Neale Fraser, John Gardiner, Brad Gilbert, Tom Gorman, Dick Gould, Jack Groppel, Heinz Gunthardt, Billie Jean King, Chuck Kriese, Robert Lansdorp, Richard Leach, Jim Loehr, Clarence Mabrey, Vioral Marcu, Arthur Marshall, George McCall, John McEnroe, Patrick McEnroe, Greg Moran, John Newcombe, Ian Occleshaw, Tony Palafox, Tony Roche, Ray Ruffles, Wally Rutter, Nick Saviano, Brian Slattery, Don Tregonning, Alice Tym, Bill Tym, Dennis Van der Meer.

Referees and Umpires:

Peter Bellenger, Flo Blanchard, Mike Blanchard, Gayle

Bradshaw, Brian Earley, Jim Entink, Frank Hammond, Lee Jackson, Jeremy Shales, Jack Starr.

Media:

Russ Adams, Neil Amdur, Don Baker, John Barrett, Peter Bodo, Ron Bookman, Jack Canon, Mary Carillo, Ron Casey, Jimmy Cefalo, Bud Collins, Allison Danzig, Richard Evans, Ed Fabricius, Steve Flink, Charles "Chuck" Friedman, Howard Gill, Bob Greene, Greg Hobbs, Murray Janoff, George Kalinsky, Don Lawrence, Barry Lorge, Igor Makurin, George McGann, Alex McNab, Paul Mellor, Barry Newcome, John Parsons, Linda Pentz, Ken Pickens, Al Picker, Chip Reid, Gene Scott, Doug Smith, Dick Squires, Michael Stevens, Alan Trengrove, Jack Wilkinson, Richard Yallop, Harold Zimman.

Special Events:

American Express—Warner Canto, Maurice Segal. Avon—Bill Corbett. Madison Square Garden—Ella Musolino. People To People Sports—Leonard Milton. New York Junior Tennis League—Skip Hartman. Petersville Products—James McCoy. Remington Products—Tory Kiam, Victor Kiam. Rolex Watch U.S.A.—Rene Dentan, Roland Puton, Bill Sullivan.

Celebrities and VIPs:

Richard Branson, Oleg Cassini, Bart Davis, David Dinkins, Charlton Heston, William Hudnut III, Alan King,

Fred Perry, Alexander Shields, William Simon, Sergio Tacchini, Ted Tingling, Diane Von Furstenberg, Fred Wilpon.

Champions in Other Sports:

Basketball—Lou Carnesecca, Nancy Lieberman. Boxing—Lionel Rose, Alan Rudkin. Cricket—Colin McDonald. Golf—Arnold Palmer, Peter Thompson. Lawn Bowls—Alec Eames. Squash—Geoff Hunt, Roshan Khan. Table Tennis—Karol Javor, Suzie Javor.

And the hundreds of great athletes representing thirty-seven sports, I was privileged to rub shoulders with at the United States Olympic Committee Sports Festivals in 1979, '81, '82 and '83.

Thank you to all those named and unnamed, who contributed to my tennis career.

22

Henry Christian Hopman

Henry "Harry" Hopman, also sometimes called "Hop" or "The Fox", was born on December 8th 1906, in Sydney, Australia.

Twenty-two years later, he burst onto the international tennis scene and commenced a remarkable career that would distinguish him as a player, Davis Cup captain, administrator, sports columnist and world class coach.

Perhaps his greatest achievement was molding the teams that would bring 16 Davis Cup victories to Australia. His unprecedented era as captain started in 1938 and 1939 as a player. After World War Two he continued his captaincy for an unbroken 19 years, ranging from 1950 to 1968. No other Davis Cup captain has been able to put together such a record, and I do not expect that anyone ever will in the future.

He was known as a fitness fanatic, believing that if all else was equal between players, fitness would become the deciding factor in achieving a win.

He had the ability to bring out the maximum amount of stamina in his players with a well controlled fitness program. He believed in it so much that there was no room on his team for someone who could not go the maximum distance in a match.

The nickname of "The Fox" came about by his uncanny

sense of being able to discern a player's weakness and translate that information to his team in a well-thought-out process. Sometimes that would be to break down an opposition's strength, leaving that player with a devastating mental quandary. His deadpan look never gave away his thoughts, or his emotions, as he carefully planned his line of attack.

In 1970, he moved to the United States where he became a dominant force in working with world class players, and those who strived to join that group.

He opened his own Harry Hopman's International Tennis Academy in Florida in 1976, where he remained until his death in 1985.

It was my great privilege to work by his side during my tenure at the Lawn Tennis Association of Victoria in Australia, where he was the president, and again in the United States, before he ventured out on his own.

His academy continues to thrive and his methods and ideals are the forefront of the programs offered to those who attend.

Many books could be written on the life of this icon, but that is for someone with more talent than I.

In the meantime, this great legend of tennis lives on in our memories.

23

Volunteering

For over fifty years I was a volunteer for various clubs, organizations and all sorts of entities often wondering why, on some occasions, I had put myself in the position of having to make a choice of doing something for my own end, or fulfilling the obligation that I had committed to for another cause. There was no doubt that if I was going to be a serious volunteer, then that task was equally as important as my own desire. So it has been for all of these years, a journey in helping someone who needs help, playing a role in making an event successful, delivering a meal to a person who is homebound or just being there when needed. The rewards are great and each thank you is like a gift of gold.

Tennis would not be the game it is today if it were not for volunteers and there are plenty of opportunities for those who want to get involved. Even the big tournaments have a band of volunteers alongside the professional staff to help organize the event.

Volunteering is a crucial part of any organization and if it were not for those who dedicate themselves to helping with administration, developing flyers, sending out notices, providing transportation and the million other things that come up, many grass roots programs would not get off the ground.

What does it mean to be a volunteer? The following might help you decide if it is right for you.

Desire

First you have to have the desire. This means that you need to have an interest in the organization, club, association or group that you are volunteering for. Perhaps you have children involved, which is often the case, or maybe you just have an interest in "playing your part." Whatever the reason, you must want to do it.

Time

If you have the desire, you must also have the time. Most volunteers simply say yes when they are asked, without knowing how much time they can give. It is a good idea to say to your organizers: "I have X hours of time per week or month, my best days are so and so. What can I do for you in that time frame?" Knowing what they have at their disposal allows the organizers to plan around your availability.

Commitment

Having made known your desire and time available, you must now fulfill your commitment. The person responsible for coordinating all volunteers must now work out the program to include everyone's time frame. A lot of effort and hours go into this task and if the truth be known, probably another volunteer is doing it.

The worst thing that can happen is that plans are made

and distributed among the work force and at the last minute someone decides that they have a dentist appointment, a hairdo to have done, a tennis or racquetball game, or a golf game came up at the last minute, precluding you from carrying out your task. This is like breaking a link in a chain and it cannot be fixed on the spot. Remember when you offer to do something you are also making a commitment to carry out your promise. Of course, emergencies happen and these cannot be helped but let your organizer know promptly so that a new link can be put in the chain. If you have pre-determined appointments that conflict, notify him or her well in advance.

Cost

Take into account the cost of your commitment. Most volunteers do not consider that it can cost them some money to be a volunteer. Gasoline, vehicle wear and tear, small purchases, donations etc., all add up. Be prepared to invest at least a few dollars to do your job. Some organizations are able to reimburse for out-of-pocket expenses. Some are not. Do not expect it, and it will not be a downer. It all goes with the territory.

Reward

There is no financial reward for being a volunteer. Make sure you understand this before you make the commitment. It is a labor of love. The whole idea of volunteering is to have "no cost helpers" do the work so that the overall financial burden of the task at hand is lessened. Your reward is the satisfaction of having played a role in achieving the goal of your club, association or organization.

I urge you to be a volunteer, even if only in a small way, it is a real experience.

24
Remington International Family Tennis Championships

Perhaps the largest ever family tennis competition to be conceived on a worldwide basis got off to a very humble start.

The brainchild of Victor Kiam, President and Chief Executive Officer of Remington Products Inc., makers of electric shavers and other fine personal products, first explored his passion for family tennis by inviting friends to participate in a father/son get-together for some experimental competition. The experiment was so successful that an annual tournament was about to begin in the United States, under the company name.

However, the first Remington program was introduced in Great Britain in 1985 by Victor Kiam and tennis buff Henry Wancke of Abbot Media Services, and it flourished to the extent of eventually having sixteen regions of the country participating. Perhaps its success was partly due to the fact that a longstanding family tennis program was already in existence in the country, and that made it a sound foundation for the Remington program to build on.

It was inevitable that a similar program would get started in the United States and that Britain and the United States would have to meet each other in a play-off, and so the Kiam Cup was established.

January of 1987 saw the first Remington International

Teams Challenge competition between these two countries come into fruition. Each team would be comprised of four father/son pairings, and the neutral venue for the play-off was selected to be held at the La Manga Club, Los Belones, Spain. The Kiam Cup competition was on its way.

With Wancke in the media field, word spread about the success of the event and other nations began to inquire as to how they could participate. Henry took on the role of tournament director and soon programs were put into place in Australia, Canada, Czechoslovakia, The Federal Republic of Germany, Japan, Korea and New Zealand, who would now join Great Britain and the United States. These countries would compete in the second Kiam Cup World Finals competition. The tournament which now had added an individual father/son and legends event was played again in Spain, at the Tennis Club of Las Brisas in Marbella, over the dates of February 20–27th, 1988. International rules of play were adopted, and the spirit of family union was predominant from start to finish.

The appeal of such a tournament was growing rapidly, and the number of participating nations grew to twelve in 1989 and to sixteen in 1990. The growth rate was phenomenal and the number of players trying to gain representation of their country for the World Finals reached a staggering thirty-four thousand individuals. To say that people from all corners of the world were coming together for a family tennis tournament was not exaggeration. The nations that had run their own national programs first and would now prepare for this multi-national get-together in 1990 were Australia, Canada, Czechoslovakia, The Federal Republic of Germany, Great Britain, Hungary, Israel, Japan, New Zealand, The People's Republic of China, Portugal, Puerto Rico, Sweden, Switzerland, The Union of Soviet Socialist Republics and The United States of America.

The program had now grown to include not only the Kiam Cup, the Father/Son and Legends—but to complete the true family picture, a Mother/Daughter division.

I first became involved with Remington when in May of 1988 I received a telephone call from Tory Kiam, Victor's son and partner on the court. We reminisced over times when I had, as president of the Eastern Tennis Association, presented him and his father with championship father/son awards and to him personally, a good sportsmanship award.

However, I realized that the purpose of his call was not to just relive old times, but that he wanted to tell me how successful their family tennis championships were. They needed help with the administration and organization of what was fast becoming a revolution in family tennis. Would I be interested in being part of the team?

After a series of talks and negotiations, I took on the role of USA tournament director and International coordinator for the Remington International Family Tennis Championships.

My first task was to set up a tournament that would allow mother/daughter and father/son teams to compete for a national championship. The winners would automatically represent the United States in the World Finals to be played in the early part of the following year. Entries would be received from any team in the country that wanted to participate. The days of "invitational" teams except for the Legends were over. This format would now ensure that the best teams in these categories would be our representatives at the international meeting.

Through my various contacts, I was successful in negotiating to have the Maryland Farm Racquet Club in Nashville, Tennessee become our host club for both the 1988 and

1989 national events. The tournament would be held in September of each year.

Entries came from all parts of the United States, and seeing these families coming together, not only to compete on the court, but to share their bonds of parental union, was an experience that will long be remembered.

Our first national championship provided us with the teams to represent our country at the International Championships scheduled to be played April 15th through the 22nd 1989, at Club Intersport, Centro Cadro, Lugano, Switzerland.

Nations that had joined our program since the previous year, were Israel, Portugal, Sweden, Switzerland, and for the first time ever to participate in an international family tournament, the USSR.

Incidentally, Australasia (Australia and New Zealand combined) played in the 1988 and 1989 Kiam Cup team championships, but played as individual nations in other events. In 1990 however, they would play as separate nations in all events that they entered.

On our entry into Lugano airport, which was a bumpy approach in a light aircraft, and one that you did not want to look through your window to see the mountains jumping up and down, the Swiss customs officials gave us our first real headache. They did not want to release the cartons that contained all of our written materials necessary to conduct the event, or the T-shirts and player gift bags. No amount of conversation would budge them and we were forced to go on to the club without our tools of trade. Fortunately, quick mediation by the local tennis officials had them on their way, and we were able to breathe easier.

How we got through that week I will never know. We were plagued by rain that caused delay after delay and I am sure it was the wettest week of out-door tennis play that any of us had encountered. Full praise must go to Henry Wancke our tournament director and Jeremy Shales our referee, who with their staff and the staff of the club, worked tirelessly day and night making the adjustments necessary to finish the tournament and crown our champions.

Another coup for the championships was that the International Tennis Federation sanctioned the event in 1990. This was the first time that the I.T.F. had sanctioned an event of this kind, and they acknowledged that the promotion and growth of the game that this program had generated, justified its position on the global tennis calendar.

Marjorie and I stayed on for a few days after the conclusion of our hectic week to enjoy the surroundings and catch our breath. When it was time to leave, we thought about the flight in, and decided a repeat performance of those aerodynamics must be avoided. We opted for the train ride back to Zurich, which was magnificent. The actual sight of those fairy tale postcards of the Swiss Alps, in real life, put us in awe of the way Mother Nature performs her artistry.

During the next few months new national programs were put into place in Australia, Hungary, New Zealand, The People's Republic of China, Portugal and Puerto Rico; bringing the number of nations participating in the Remington International Family Tennis Championships to sixteen. International Family Tennis competition was truly on the way up, and Remington was at the forefront of promoting this great spectacle.

Bringing these nations closer together as families had indeed created a better understanding of each other's cultures, and served to help solve some of the international problems, that often seem unsolvable. When you consider that countries such as Hungary, The People's Republic of China and the USSR had not previously ventured outside of their own borders to compete in family tennis, it was amazing that the ambitious vision that Victor and Tory Kiam had for their program was consummated.

The national championships that were conducted all over the globe leading up to the 1990 International event, brought forth new champions to compete for world titles and the nations that hosted them, were caught up in the excitement of who would be successful.

The United States was designated to be the host nation of the 1990 International World Finals and I made arrangements to stage our tournament at the fabulous Club Med Sandpiper Village in Port St. Lucie, Florida, over the dates of April 21st to 28th. The program would consist of the Kiam Cup, an International team event for father/son and mother/daughter pairs representing their countries; the Remington International father/son, mother/daughter championships, for the world's best pairings in those categories; and the Legends, for invited father/son pairs with the father having to be at least sixty years of age. We also planned to run an unofficial mixed doubles event if time permitted, and the demand was definitely there. All told, there were one hundred and fifty teams from around the globe competing for the honor of world champion.

As the host facility, I can only say that Club Med did an outstanding job. Their experience in catering to multinational groups throughout the world was a plus factor, providing a grand experience for everyone. Their staff staged outstanding entertainment during off-court hours and looked after every detail necessary for us to run our event, which again was under the guidance of Wancke and Shales.

To highlight the event and spread the word about the program throughout the United States and abroad, we arranged for the television taping of the Championships from start to finish. The film was distributed through the Viacom network which reached over sixty million viewers.

It was hoped that a presenting sponsorship could be found to help defray costs of this ever growing tournament. While we had some minor sponsors that helped with reduced air fares, accommodation and tennis balls, for which we were most appreciative, it was not enough to make the financial burden manageable.

Part of my role as International Coordinator was to try and obtain sponsorship, but in the words of another (always solo) sport, "I had some fish on the hook occasionally, but they all got away." Well—you can't win them all.

Perhaps it was unfortunate that the financial burden became unbearable and that this program that had cemented so many ties between countries, would not be continued on an international basis after 1990. In my short two years with Remington, I shared many great experiences with Victor and Tory Kiam and the people they brought together from all over the world. With more time, perhaps I could have found the resources to keep the vision growing, but we will never know.

Many of the nations involved with our vision still conduct their own programs and I am proud to have been a part of this endeavor that continues today, and which allows us to share the spirit of friendship on and off the court.

Victor Kiam said it best when he wrote:

> *The purpose of the Remington International Family Tennis Championships is not only to promote the game of tennis at the grass roots level, but more importantly, to promote strong family relationships around the world, with tennis as the common interest.*

25
Memorable Occasions

There have been so many times when I looked back over my tennis life and remembered the wonderful experiences that came my way. It is impossible to capture all of them, and sadly some will have escaped my memory. The price of getting older and not making records of the pleasures that are bestowed on us. The following are some of those occasions that linger with me.

Winning back-to-back Singles Championships in 1963–64 at my home club, in Melbourne, Australia.

Attending a session of HRH, The Duke of Edinburgh's, Third Commonwealth Study Conference, titled Industrialization and the Individual, held in Australia in 1968.

Being the administrator for the Avon Women's Futures Championships Circuit in 1973, 1974 and 1975.

Having cocktails at Tiffany's, New York, in 1974 to celebrate the founding of the *Tennis Week* newspaper, now turned magazine.

Being listed in the 1978 *Tennis Week* magazine's "Who's Who" of men's professional tournament directors. The list depicted 42 directors representing 50-odd events.

Representing Australians Living in America, in Men's Senior International Teams Championship competition, The Stevens Cup, in 1980, 1981, 1982, 1983 and 1984.

Raising $20,000 for the National Kidney Foundation,

using a Challenge Tennis Match between the ice hockey giants, the Islanders and the Rangers, in 1981.

Representing Tennis Australia in the Davis Cup semi-final draw for play, in Portland, Oregon, USA in 1981. Marvin Richmond, President of the U.S.T.A. drew Mark Edmondson of Australia, and yours truly drew John McEnroe of the U.S. to play the first rubber.

Being listed in the 1983 publication of the International "Who's Who" in Tennis.

Receiving the 1992 Tennis Man of the Year award from the Eastern Tennis Association in New York, USA.

Being a recipient (with my wife Marjorie), of a Special Husband and Wife Service Award from the Newtown Tennis Association (Connecticut, USA) in 1997.

Accepting the Tennis Family of the Year Award with Marjorie and our three sons, Perry, Grant and Scott, from the Eastern Tennis Association, USA, in 1997.

Acting as tournament director for five years to the Sweethearts Tennis Tournament in New York. The tournament, a charity event that raises funds for the Juvenile Diabetes Foundation, has produced over one million dollars for this cause in its history.

Being inducted into the Newtown (Connecticut, USA) Sports Hall of Fame in 2001.

Receiving the honor of being inducted into the United States/Eastern Tennis Hall of Fame in 2002. The ceremony was held at the United Nations, New York, USA.

Playing as part of the team that won the U.S.T.A. Super Senior New England League Doubles Championships Triple Crown in 2002, 2003 and 2004. What an experience to play with these guys who play hard but fair, and have a lot of fun doing it. The team members were: Henry Blodgett (my partner, we were undefeated in three years), Jim Carley, Ken Coley, Will Cravens, Arthur Goldblatt, Mike

Gorman, Pete Harrity, Jim Krauser, Dom Nocturne, Bob Schneider (our captain) and Tom Walker.

Being a tennis consultant, and doing the tennis tips for the Pete Summers television show, "Tennis Talk" in 2004, shown over the Charter and Comcast TV networks.

Writing this book.

26
A Brush with Death—Part Two

It was 8:20 A.M. on October 20th, 1984, and I was on my way to the Port Washington Tennis Academy on Long Island, New York to commence my duties there for the day as the C.E.O. and General Manager. My home was about 3 miles from the Academy and I was planning on an 8:30 A.M. start and getting ready for another 10–14 hour session.

I had reached the four-way stop sign at the intersection, just three doors from my house, which would take me to the facility, and after stopping, looked right, looked left, looked right again and not seeing any traffic, moved into the center of the intersection to make my left turn. Suddenly, all hell broke loose! Out of nowhere I was struck on the left side of my car just at the separating pillar between the front and back seats. A vehicle had run the stop sign to my left, and also wanted, as I found out later, to make a left turn at this same intersection.

The police report later established that the driver was taking his son to his SATs, had forgotten something and was rushing back home to retrieve it.

The impact sent my car spinning down the road about thirty to forty feet and we both finished up facing each other in opposite directions, blocking the whole roadway.

Fortunately I was wearing my seat belt, but even so, the left side of my head hit the pillar, then jerked backward and to the right until my head was almost resting on my right shoulder. I was still conscious but experiencing pain in the neck and shoulder regions. The driver of the other car and his son, who were unhurt, came running over to see if I was alright. I was able to tell them where I lived, and to please report the accident to my wife and get ambulance and police help.

Before long, my wife and youngest son Scott arrived, and shortly after the ambulance and police. After a brief evaluation, I was taken to the hospital some ten minutes away, where, in the emergency room, I was examined and put under heavy sedation for the weekend. As I still had some mobility I was sent home at the end of the day and an appointment was made to visit my personal doctor on Monday, where X-rays were taken and a thorough examination was completed. It was established that I had a severe whiplash. Instead of the natural curve of the cervical area of the spine, my fate was to have that natural curve twisted into an "S" shape, which was causing considerable pain to that upper area. Therapy was applied immediately along with injections, anti-inflammatory medication and pain pills, all of which would go on for many months.

In March of 1985 I was required to attend a United States Tennis Association annual meeting in Scottsdale, Arizona. The flight required a connection in Atlanta, and while we were waiting in the lounge for our aircraft, I was struck with a severe stabbing pain in the neck. It was so sharp I was sure someone had stabbed me with a knife, but on turning around, no one was there. Soon a severe headache began and stayed with me throughout the rest of the trip despite the pills I was "popping." I was definitely not a good traveling companion for Marjorie.

The U.S.T.A. annual meeting is a non stop series of meetings, and on this occasion I was destined not to attend any of them. The pain became excruciating and I owe a great debt to our friend Susan, the wife of a colleague, who spent hours massaging my neck and shoulders, providing me with relief.

On March 26th I was taken to see a Dr. James Nichols in Phoenix, a well-known orthopedic surgeon, and father of a promising up and coming tennis player, Bruce Nichols. Dr. Nichols examined me, took X-rays, and after consultation with my physician in New York, Dr. Irving Glick, advised my immediate return to New York for probable surgery. I was referred to a number of doctors for evaluation, and by April 2nd I had lost the mobility in my right shoulder and arm. On April 4th I was admitted to the North Shore Community Hospital on Long Island for surgery, and put under the care of two neuro-surgeons. I might add that April 4th is my wedding anniversary and it was not much of a day for my wife. The tests started all over again in preparation for the surgery and after about 10 hours of every test imaginable, the last one for the day was a myelogram. I can recall that the time was about 9 P.M. when the first results came through and were not clear due to the fact that I had unknowingly moved my right arm. The result was that a second injection of dye was necessary, which unfortunately made me extremely sick and gave me head pain so intense that I wanted to dig my eyes out of their sockets. I was in a semi-private ward and the noise of turning a book page by the man sharing the room with me, sounded like all the banshees from hell.

Needless to say, surgery was postponed and medication administered to relieve the pain. For six days the doctors tried different drugs but without success. I was beginning to reach the end of my endurance. April 10th came and they tried another drug called Elavil, a powerful anti-inflammatory—and it worked. The pain in my neck and shoulders subsided, and surgery was cancelled. Therapy was commenced immediately and I was discharged from the hospital on April 13th under the care of Dr. Glick. The diagnosis by the hospital was R/O compression of the cervical cord between the fifth & sixth vertebrae.

The attention that Dr. Glick would give to my rehabilitation and the patience that he would show went far beyond my expectations. I was firmly convinced that I would never play tennis again, for after all, I had this thing hanging down my side that was useless. Dr. Glick had other ideas. One day when working on my mobility, he said, "I think it is time for you to hit some tennis balls."

I was outraged; how could I hit a tennis ball in my condition? I was soon to learn a great lesson: Never Give Up.

We went to the locker room where my racket was taped to my right hand with sports tape. "How is this going to help?" I asked, "My racket is dragging on the ground."

My friend looked at me and said; "If you pick up your right hand with your left hand it will no longer be on the ground." He taught me how to hit with two hands, not well at first, but I did master it eventually, and even learned to serve two-handed overheads. He worked with me week after week and month after month, patiently exercising my body and my mind, until my confidence returned and I was able to play once more. My spirit had been rejuvenated and my will to beat the problem had been established. My recovery was about 85 percent plus and even now sometimes I pull out a two-hander from either side of the body, and smile at the look on my opponents faces.

In 1990, six years after the accident, a settlement of $250,000 was agreed to by the insurance company of the other driver who had hit me, but in no way does that compensate for the pain and suffering that is mine for life.

December of 1994 saw the surgery needed, the same

surgery that had been cancelled in 1985, when the disc between cervical five and six disintegrated. Surgery was successful, but therapy continues for the rest of my life.

One of the beautiful things about moving to Newtown, Connecticut, was the change in environment and the slower pace so vastly different from New York City and its surroundings. We were fortunate to find a magnificent home on more than two acres which gave us the opportunity to do our own gardening and landscaping. We had looked at places both closer to and further away from New York, but none were appealing. We liked space around us and a quieter country town atmosphere. Our real estate agent found exactly what we were looking for: privacy, a water view, rolling hills, a home just eight years old needing no work, and lots of land to satisfy the most ardent gardener, nestled in a rural setting. It was perfect Here was land to be tilled into garden beds, rocks to be used for landscaping and enough to do around the house to keep us going for years to come. This was not viewed as hard labor, as I always looked at these tasks as an exercise program, and to this day, still enjoy doing these things around the house with my wife and companion.

On June 21st of 2000 I was cutting the lawn. It was hot and humid and the task usually took me about an hour to complete. I was about half way through the job and suddenly felt fatigued, which was unusual, but I had to stop and rest. In a few minutes I completed my lawn cutting, and again felt drained. I had not felt like this before and had always been proud of the fact that I was able to sustain long work periods, just like sustaining long rallies in a tennis match. I put it down to the weather and refreshed myself in the shower.

The next day I was giving a tennis lesson and again felt

the feeling of acute fatigue. I decided it was time to call my doctor. His advice was, that if the feeling had not subsided in 5 minutes, to get to the emergency room at the hospital and have someone call him, and he would meet me there. If, however, I felt better, to come to his office which was just 10 minutes away. Well, I recovered and felt that I could drive, so off I went for an examination. He soon released me to the care of a cardiologist and many tests were done over the next few days. The final result being that I had a 97 percent blockage in the left coronary artery and immediate surgery was required. The procedure was to have a "stent" inserted, via angioplasty, into the blocked artery, which would keep it open and regulate the blood flow to the heart. This was done successfully on July 5th and I was able to return to tennis after a short rehabilitation period.

When I think back on all these brushes with death, each one of them in the potential fatal category, it raises the adage of "the cat with nine lives." Could it be that if I were a cat I have survived seven and have two to go?

27
Tennis Consultants International, Inc.

With the disappointment of the U.S.T.A. Board failing to fulfill its promise of me heading up the newly approved player development program, I was left with a void in my tennis career. It was disturbing to say the least, that a commitment made by an outgoing president could be discarded so easily by an incoming president assuming office. There was definitely a lack of continuity in U.S.T.A. policy.

During the time that I was working on the implementation of that program and its locality, it was my good fortune to meet many people in various areas of our great game, and because of the many questions asked of me, it seemed that there was a great need for consulting services throughout the country, and perhaps even internationally. There were management companies in place that specialized in managing programs, events and players, but few consulting agencies specifically for tennis. Little did I know it at the time, but eventually we would need to get involved in management as well.

Well, a decision had to be made. *Do I look for another job, or do I work for myself and at my own pace?* Given the experiences that I had just been through with the Port Washington Tennis Academy and the United States Tennis Association, my decision was made very quickly. I would be responsible to myself and thus have no one to blame but myself, if things did not go as planned.

In October of 1987, Tennis Consultants International, Inc. was registered as a corporation. Independence had arrived and it was wonderful.

Parameters were set as to what the company could offer, and we compiled an impressive list of services. Our brochure would state that we are an exclusive tennis management and consulting company for club operation and programs, tennis tournament management, special events, charity events, tennis parties, lectures, corporate outings and marketing programs through tennis.

To be successful we needed to be able to provide answers to the many questions that would be asked, and given my experience, I was confident that this would be achieved.

Knowledge in directing and administering major tennis events such as Davis Cup, International events, Olympic and Grand Slam tournaments, circuit programs at the national, state and local levels and charity events were ingrained into my system, as were the many non-tennis spectaculars like boxing, basketball, ballet, ice-skating etc. etc.

Club management was second nature to me, having been in the chief executive officer position for one of the largest tennis clubs in Australia with over 4000 members, and the largest junior teaching academy in the United States, boasting over 1000 tennis students weekly. In addition, there were the personal membership clubs and associations that I was privileged to play in. Developing and administering the operating programs for these clubs was part of daily routine.

Giving lectures on various topics related to the game of tennis at international and national conferences, clubs, associations and organizations, and participating as a guest speaker for radio talk shows, doing television commentary and interviews, all added to our expertise. The study of the significance of sports medicine, biomechanics, fitness, nutrition and psychology as it relates to athletics, and the wellbeing of the human body, both physically and mentally, enlarged our capacity to deal with the individual whose goals were infinite. Finally, but not limiting our ability to learn more ourselves, we studied the need for efficient designing of buildings that would house sporting activities, and the utilization of that space combined with attractive décor and landscaping.

Consulting for over 40 years to corporations, organizations, associations, clubs and individuals, has provided us with in-depth relationships with high visibility individuals, world class players, and the development of programs necessary for these entities to pursue successful marketing ventures. Many sponsorships were found for tennis through these partnerships, and the game of tennis has benefited from our efforts.

Being a teacher of tennis where one gets to show the student the fundamentals of the game and help that student to master them, is a satisfying experience. What surpasses that experience, is becoming the coach of that student who having learned the skills, now needs advice on how to apply them.

All of this activity know-how is what the company is all about, and we are proud to have been given the opportunity to share our knowledge with those who have sought us out.

Our partial list of major achievements and corporate associations include:

The American Express Challengers Circuit.
The Avon Futures Circuit.
The Rolex International Junior Championships.
The Remington International Family Championships.

The Mayor's Cup, High School Championships, New York.
The Sweethearts Tennis Championships for Juvenile Diabetes, New York.
The Newtown Open Tennis Championships, Connecticut.
Consulting to the United States Tennis Association.
Consulting to Parks and Recreation Departments.
Consulting to Sports Technique and Reaction Training Systems.
Consulting for the establishment of an International Tennis Training Facility in Great Britain.
Consultant/Coach for university-level tennis teams.
Representing Tennis Australia in the United States.
Representing the Australian Davis Cup Foundation in the United States.

At the time of writing, we continue to be part of the great game of tennis in our small way, and eagerly await the challenges that confront us in the years to come.

28

Beaver Brook Tennis Club

Twelve months after we had sold our house in the prestigious area of Sands Point on Long Island, New York, we moved to Connecticut where we had found a home in Newtown, a quiet country town between New York and Boston, nestled in the spectacular landscape of New England. Our new home provided us with the majority of comforts that one looks for when planning semi-retirement. The year was 1992. Well—semi-retirement never came, and is still somewhere around the corner, but I am still working on it.

By early summer of 1992 we had seen the settling in period of a new house go by, although there were plenty of boxes in the basement still to be unpacked, and Marjorie and I decided to look for a place to play tennis. We visited a number of clubs in the area to see what they had to offer and finished up at the Beaver Brook Tennis Club in Danbury, as the last one on the list for that day. We were greeted by a very pleasant receptionist named Beth who gave us the answers to all of our questions and in turn asked us about our tennis history. Soon she had referred us to the owner, but not before quietly mentioning to him the fish she had on the hook out front, and that the club was short a teaching "pro" for their program the next day. We were shown around the club by the owner, Jon, and were impressed with the overall facility and the friendliness of the staff.

At the end of our tour, Jon, who had shown great restraint about the need for a "pro" the next day, asked me if I would be interested in helping out with his problem. Having liked what I had seen, I agreed, and next morning walked onto the court, and gave my first lesson at the Beaver Brook Tennis Club.

This was the start of my eleven-year experience at this club.

My time there is filled with many fond memories and friendships that were created with staff and customers alike. There is probably enough material in that period alone to make a great story.

What made this club a great experience was the friendly atmosphere that was created by the ownership. Jon and his wife Janet really understood what a partnership needed to do to create success. Their approach to the customer was from the old school, that being: the customer is always right, even if they are wrong. Diplomacy was used to eliminate dissatisfaction and to solve problems. The customers were always given a good hearing and ample time to express their concerns. Obviously, there were always some disagreements, but these were usually sorted out amicably and the work of teaching tennis went on.

One such unpleasant experience, which happened to be staff-related, took place when I was asked to give up some of my adult students so that an incoming professional would have some teaching hours. My personal concept was, and still is, that if you are coming in as a new teacher, you built up your hours by being around and available. When I started, that's what I had to do, and I was peeved at this new philosophy. Not that I had anything against the new guy, but I was disappointed at the way the owner had handled it. I never really made a fuss about it and worked hard at keeping harmony within the teaching ranks. Completely unaware of how things had happened, our new teacher, who was an excellent player and coach, quickly became part of the family and a good friend of mine, and that friendship remains to this day.

My position as a professional tennis teacher at Beaver Brook was an extremely rewarding experience, being able to work with both adult and junior players, imparting my knowledge of the game and its complexities to all levels of players. The greatest satisfaction a teacher can receive is to see the student absorb the context of the subject, be courageous enough to try it out, and achieve putting that context into fruition.

There is nothing like the light in a student's eyes and the smile on his or her face, when the line has been crossed in achieving success. When you see that, you know that you have performed well as a teacher. Unfortunately, a lot of so-called teachers today are only in it for the money and I would say to them; learn your subject before you teach it and you will receive greater rewards than money can provide.

My duties also included administration, part of which was designing lesson formats, setting up class content, which I always did on an ability-level basis irrespective of gender, but sometimes taking age into account, and then finally allocating the teaching staff to those classes. These teachers would be rotated every few weeks to insure that the students received the maximum benefits from the knowledge that each of them had to impart.

In addition, I devised and ran special tournaments, introduced an intense training program for advanced players under the heading of *Sports Technique and Reaction Training*, assisted in the planning of adult clinics and lesson programs, formatted and directed league competition, etc., etc., etc. I was completely happy in my "bubble."

During the latter part of 2001, Jon and Janet announced that they had sold the club and new ownership would be coming in almost immediately. It came as such a surprise to everyone as it was a well known fact that the club was successful and financially stable; however, there were personal reasons that had prompted the sale and after more than 28 years of ownership, the time had come to enjoy life and family to the fullest elsewhere.

The new owners came in at the beginning of the fall semester and immediately started to re-organize. Old files and records were tossed out and new ones created, causing a feeling of uncertainty about the future with the staff, and speculation was prominent due to lack of information. Here was a group of dedicated people who were accustomed to a healthy family-style operation with character and good member relations, suddenly learning that the real business world had arrived. Unfortunately, there was never any real communication to the staff or membership as to what the plans were, so imagination ran rampant, resulting in dissatisfied members and a lack of confidence throughout the club.

We all know that when one buys a new business or a new home, or whatever, one has the right to run it and furnish it according to one's desires and goals, but not to make those plans available to the personnel that can make it happen, borders on stupidity. Anyhow, new management was appointed, but their talents were soon divided between Beaver Brook and other ventures that our new owners were involved in. Staff was still looking for direction.

From a personal point of view, I was asked to assist in administration by running a 150-player in-house league program, set up a U.S.T.A. league team and training program which became a 5 team 80 player effort, assist the tennis director by setting up teaching classes, meet students and parents on arrival, make sure students were on the correct courts on time, distribute performance prizes etc., etc. In addition, I was the front man for parents and members to talk to if they had a problem, which I would solve or pass on to management. I would help the desk staff, answer the telephone, sell rackets, fold towels, replenish locker room supplies, keep the place tidy and do anything else that came my way.

Due to these demands I was asked to give up some of my teaching hours. This related to less earnings, as administrative hours were at a lower rate than teaching hours, and it would become a pattern for cost cutting and eventual replacement of staff whom ownership considered to be too highly paid. One of their methods of recruiting teachers was to offer U.S. Visa sponsorship, thus helping applicants get through the maze of immigration laws. As a result, many foreign professionals apply, and they are happy to work for a lesser amount than the homeland guy, in order to get a U.S. permit and Visa.

I had become accustomed to my new role in administration and felt I was playing the part that had been set up for me, when in March of 2003 I was informed that 10 of my admin. hours had been cut immediately. This meant dropping the junior program and all of its related activities. It was embarrassing explaining to the juniors and their parents why this great part of our program was no longer in existence. May brought further notification that all of my admin-hours were at an end, and I was now no longer looking after U.S.T.A. League teams, and in addition, when I checked the court sheets I noticed that I had been taken off the teaching part of that program. No communication, no discussion, nothing, just replacement by a lesser paid professional.

I certainly understand the need to cut costs, particularly

when things get out of hand, and I believe they did in some areas, but the methods used here were completely unprofessional and hurt many of the loyal staff who had made this club successful. Hardly any of the original group remains today.

Membership also was affected with back-to-back increases in January and September of 2002 and again in September of 2003, resulting in loss of long time supporters to other clubs, and in some cases to tennis. It was with regret that I resigned in June of ~~1993~~ 2003.

Plans to turn the club into a multi-sport complex had not come into fruition at the time of writing.

29

Newtown Tennis Association

Not long after we had settled into our new home in Newtown, Connecticut and I had started working full-time as a teaching professional at the Beaver Brook Tennis Club, I learned of a meeting being held at the club by the Newtown Tennis Association.

While my wife and I were looking for a house in Newtown our real estate agent had mentioned how much the town was orientated toward tennis, among other things, and we decided that it might be interesting to learn about this organization first hand.

We duly went to the meeting and there were about twenty or so people present. We found that the gathering was in fact their annual general meeting. It would take the form of business first, followed by social tennis. A great idea, this got people together.

Having been accustomed to large attendances of up to one hundred at association meetings in Australia, it seemed rather strange to us that this meeting would have so few attendees. We soon learned that this was in fact an association of people, and not of clubs as we knew it.

The format was simple; a brief report by the president on the activities from the previous year and a report from the treasurer on the financial status. As the last item of business, the president remarked that a new president was required. The thrust of the discussion seemed to be, "Let's get this over with and get on the court."

After very few words, and much silence, suddenly out of nowhere the treasurer stood up and said, "I would like to nominate Alex Aitchison for the position." I nearly fell off my chair. Neither Marjorie or myself were members—and surely I was not eligible. The treasurer went on to say that he had information about my tennis background and that I was more than qualified for the position. He asked me to give the members a brief presentation of my experience. Having done that, I made a comment that I thought it would be more appropriate if someone with greater longevity in the town be elected.

After a call for further nominations, which was followed by more silence, someone seconded the treasurer's nomination, and the chairman quickly said, "All those in favor, against, carried," and I was the president, effective immediately. A quick wrap-up led to the courts and a good time was had by all. That was in 1994 and I held that position through 1995 and 1996.

At the time, I thought that this could not be too bad, seeing that this is a group of people numbering about fifty, and to organize their playing needs should not be too onerous. In addition, Jon Bloom, the owner of the Beaver Brook Tennis Club, offered me the resources of the club to help in my administration.

My first duty, for my own benefit, was to establish how the association ran, what its structure was, and what its activities were. The treasurer and secretary had not been opposed at the meeting and therefore stayed on board. I was able to learn from them.

Meetings had been haphazard and only called when it was necessary to make decisions that could not be made by telephone communication.

The activity list consisted of three tournaments, The Newtown Open, which was open to any player from anywhere; the Bertram Stroock Memorial Championships, which was limited to Newtown residents only, and the Junior Stroock, also limited to locals.

These and three or four tennis party nights at the Beaver Brook club during the indoor season, just about made up the events that had to be organized. These nights were great social get-togethers where the members brought an array of favorite foods and the association provided refreshments.

Most other tennis played was by mutual agreement between the members, on the thirteen courts, spread over three locations maintained by the Newtown Parks and Recreation Department, and in the fine weather months, it was often difficult to get a court.

My concept of what an association should be and what its role was, differed greatly from what I was seeing. There were differences however. This one being for individuals, and, my experience being for clubs that catered for many more members. There were no clubs in Newtown though, and it was not unreasonable to apply the same principles that I knew, to this organization.

I sat down and planned a structure and goals list.

First we needed to form a proper management committee consisting of President, Vice President, Treasurer and Secretary, all to be elected. Added to this group would be a tournament chairman, social secretary, press officer and a legal adviser appointed by the president.

Secondly, it was important to write and adopt a constitution coupled with by-laws. I had been able to uncover some rules governing play but discovered nothing laid out about the associations responsibilities and goals, the election process, or the protection of funds generated from membership dues, tournament income or sponsorship.

We also needed to increase our membership base. A larger membership would provide additional revenue to help offset costs of administration.

An important part of our operation would be to provide membership benefits such as sandlot tennis, where players could come down to the courts as an individual and pick up a game, have BBQs combined with social play with the association providing both food and refreshments, free adult and junior clinics under the guidance of volunteers, create a junior travel team to represent Newtown at no cost to the players, and lastly but not least, seek sponsorship from local merchants to further enhance our tournaments and clinics.

A grandiose plan? Yes, but I felt confident that it was workable if we could get the local newspaper, the *Newtown Bee*, to help us, and they did.

Our press officer churned out press releases about our every move, which the paper printed, and eventually they gave us a weekly column under our own name and logo. This did wonders for getting our message out, and soon the membership list grew to some one hundred families representing about two hundred and eighty individuals.

This activity raised the interest level in the tennis community and with the extra funds from membership dues we were able to start providing the benefits we had promised. Saturday morning clinics became a regular thing, organized social play followed by a BBQ became a fun thing and fostered social integration, a challenge ladder was created and a junior travel team was put into place.

All the while, we were working on the constitution and by-laws and eventually presented it to the membership who adopted it unanimously. This now meant that the association and its officers were protected, the monies it generated were protected, as were all of the events that we would conduct.

So far as I could establish, the annual Newtown Open had a long and illustrious history going back to 1975. Many exciting matches had been fought out on the hard courts of Newtown during this time. It really is the highlight of the tennis year for the Association with the finals being played in the early part of June. Preliminary rounds are played during the preceding six to eight weeks where the players arrange their own times and places. Each round, however, must be completed within a time frame set by the tournament committee. There are eleven divisions all told, including open men's and women's singles and doubles and mixed doubles, plus forty and over and fifty and over divisions complementing the event. At its peak, the tournament has had as many as three hundred and fifty plus entries with players coming from within a fifty-mile radius of Newtown. My goal was to upgrade the calibre of the event by making it more attractive and an event that players wanted to compete in. There was no prize money, so it had to be appealing in some other way.

The Bertram Stroock Memorial Championships and the Junior Stroock both needed a shot in the arm so far as entries were concerned. We set about boosting the enthusiasm of local players to play in these events that had been created just for them.

The secret was to promote them additionally. Through our newspaper column we got the word out about their importance to the town and soon we saw an increase in the number of participants.

To give it its own identity, the junior championships were separated from the main event and became the

Coopersmith Cup, sponsored by the two local Coopersmith families.

Eventually it would become the Victor Coopersmith Memorial Championships honoring one of the brothers who lost his life in a lake accident.

With the interest that was coming out of the junior clinics, we put together a junior travel team that would compete in the Laurel Cup inter-club competition. To help us with our expenses in this venture, the local Eagle Savings Bank provided us with an initial sponsorship that allowed us to outfit our team with T-shirts and caps showing off our mascot, the famous Newtown Rooster. Later we were fortunate to get the Western Connecticut Federal Credit Union to come on board as a full sponsor making it possible to provide coaching, clothing and travel expenses for our team. It was a great learning experience for every young player entering the competitive field.

There was still a lot to be done in promoting the game in our area and again I went to the drawing board. I needed to establish how we would pay the costs of these benefits and their administration.

I came up with what we called our "Partners Program." It was simply to get local merchants to become partners with the Association in sponsoring our various events. The arrangement would be that in return for an annual donation to the Association, we would provide a sign advertising their business. The sign would be hung on the fence of the tennis courts every time we had an official event being played.

Being that our events were conducted on town courts it was necessary to apply to the Parks and Recreation Department for permission to hang these signs. The application was dealt with promptly and was approved. I must say that during my years working on behalf of the Association, I had a wonderful rapport with Parks and Rec. and they were extremely helpful at all times. With the appropriate authority now in place, we could go out and do our selling.

My good friend, neighbor and doubles partner, Bud Miller (we won the Stroock open doubles twice together), took on the onerous task of door to door salesmen. Our efforts in pounding the pavement were rewarded with twelve businesses joining the program, providing enough funding for our needs. It was a success story from the start.

Unfortunately, due to vandalism, sometimes prevalent in public parks, it was necessary to take the signs down each day after play concluded. This required a committee of volunteers working long hours before and after each day's play, to protect our investment. I thank them all for their diligence in making my job easier. It is often forgotten that organizations such as ours literally are kept going by volunteer workers.

The biggest challenge I faced for the Association was to get sponsorship for the Newtown Open tennis tournament. It had such a long and successful history that someone must be interested, but who? It certainly would have to be local.

As luck would have it, I discovered that a member of the Beaver Brook tennis club where I worked, Darren Beylouni, was part of a family-owned Ford dealership in Danbury, Connecticut. I quickly got to know him, told him of my plan, and he arranged for me to meet his brother David, who was president of the company and personally looked after advertising and promotion. David Beylouni was a resident of Newtown, which may or may not have been a plus factor for my presentation, but I found him to be an eager listener anyhow, and he accepted my proposal.

For the first time in its history, so far as I could establish, the tournament would bear the name of a sponsor. It would be called "The Colonial Ford-Subaru Newtown Open." The year was 1998.

In return for the sponsorship, signage would be provided by us at the tournament, vehicles from the dealership would be on display, the president of the company would present the trophies, and the association would make every effort to promote the dealership through its media releases and internal news letters to its membership. In addition, part of the sponsorship fee would be used to provide a gift from the sponsor to all players competing on the last two days of the event.

Due to the success of the tournament, we procured the sponsorship again in 1999 and enjoyed even greater publicity and a huge increase in participants.

Unfortunately it was lost in 2000, when I was no longer chairman of the event, and negotiations broke down. The new tournament director worked for Fleet Bank and he was able to get them to pick up the sponsorship for that year. It would turn out to be the only year for Fleet, and to my knowledge no sponsorship has been obtained since.

Having lost some of the flavor that the event had for so many years, entries have also been lost to the extent that some divisions hardly can be called a draw.

It was a great experience to be the chairman from 1994 through 1999 and see the tournament make profits that could be used to sponsor the other activities of the association.

There were many people who contributed to the success of this event over those years and I thank them for making my task easier. There are too many to mention, but if you read this book, you will know who you are. I have not forgotten your efforts. However, I must pay tribute to the hard-core group who year after year were always there, unflinchingly doing what had to be done, whether it be designing entry blanks, printing the posters for distribution to clubs, accepting entries, doing the banking, doing the draws, buying the trophies, preparing the courts for play, hand writing the name plates identifying the on court players—etc., etc., etc. A special recognition to you all. Marjorie Aitchison, Lynda Doyle, Roger Giordano, Darlene Jackson, Andria Ondak, Jim Ondak, Steve Singer and Beth Wetherill. You are a great team.

After the 2000 Open was completed, and now without a sponsor, I was asked by the executive committee of the Association if my company, Tennis Consultants International Inc., would submit a proposal to conduct the tournament for future years. We did this, offering to obtain sponsorship and conduct the event on a professional basis. The powers that be decided against the proposal, and virtually turned away a guaranteed profit.

Marjorie and I fulfilled our commitment to the association through the end of the year 2000 and decided that it was time to step aside and let others "pave their own roads."

30

College Coaching

As I reached my twilight years in the game of tennis I was looking to ease my commitments to teaching and administration. My plan was to spend more time at home, play socially, and perhaps participate in an occasional tournament or two in the super senior division. I certainly was not prepared for the demanding role that teaching can often bring, that was coming my way.

During the latter part of September in 2002, I was approached by the captain of the women's team at the Western Connecticut State University. She informed me that their team for the Fall season in 2002 had collapsed. This meant they had been forced to withdraw from their competition in Division III of the Little East Conference played throughout New England.

The captain, Stacey Slater, who had been a student of mine at the Beaver Brook tennis club during her junior days, was distraught and could see her college tennis experience going down the drain if something could not be done.

The existing coach had been relieved of his duties and it was necessary to replace him if the team was to compete in 2003. "Could you help? Would you be interested in taking the position? We need you," she asked.

Another tennis student of mine, Alison Healey, also on the team, joined forces with Stacey and soon I agreed to at least meet with the athletic director.

My meeting with athletic director Ed Farrington revealed the coaching need for both the women's and men's teams. After evaluating my credentials he asked me if I would take on the responsibility of head coach for both teams, and I agreed.

Needless to say my two former students were delighted and plans to revive the roster for the fall of 2003 started to be implemented.

However, before this could happen, the men's team had to be considered and their season was coming up in the spring. I learned very quickly what had to be done and in the new year of 2003 got the word out about practice. We would need to start our practice sessions in February, continue through March, and be ready for play the first week of April.

Much to my surprise the initial roster showed ten players of high potential. It appeared that we would have a good team. About half-way through our practice period, the necessary paper work had to be filled out by the players, which included an eligibility data form. These were duly completed and handed in for processing. Well was I surprised when the results came back. We did not have a team.

In order to compete in conference matches a team must have a minimum of six players—and suddenly my roster was reduced to less than the required number. What with too many semesters (ten maximum), not enough credits, and grade point averages that were too low, our team had been dismantled unceremoniously by the rules.

No matter what we did, we were unable to come up with the required six players and again the University was forced into withdrawing from the competition.

This did not bode well for the longevity of the tennis program as overall budget cuts were forcing unfavorable decisions to eliminate those that were not successful. Here we were with six beautiful courts, three of which are lighted for night play, and no tennis teams.

In a subsequent discussion, Ed Farrington, the athletic director, took a gamble in keeping the program alive and retained me as head coach for both the men's and women's teams. These positions were both part-time and allowed him to keep the salary down as opposed to a full-time one, and it also gave me flexibility to do other things.

I very quickly realized that my position was not just to coach the players but that, recruiting had to be done, team comraderie had to be established, uniforms ordered, tennis balls procured, scorekeepers put on each of the courts, food and accommodation had to be administered on away trips, support and advice was a must when the players were on the court (not easy when all six are on at the same time), first aid administered when necessary in the absence of a trainer, words of wisdom spoken to a player who had given his/her best and come up short, and, when each match is over fax the results to the news media, help with fund raising—etc., etc.

Fall and the women's season of 2003 came around with a rush. We had built a roster of seven players adding three new prospects to the four left over from 2002. Three days before the team had to be registered, it suddenly dropped to five. I thought, *Oh, no—are we going to have a repeat of last year?*

It was a Friday afternoon and I left the practice session to advise the athletic director. He told me, "If you do not have six players by noon on Monday I cannot register the team." This was a disaster. If we withdrew two years in a row we would surely lose our women's team from the program.

I went back to the practice courts and advised the players of the situation. I told them, "I cannot do any more; if you want a team you will have to come up with at least one more player by noon on Monday."

That night, one of the players designed and produced flyers advertising our predicament and posted them on every notice board she could find on campus. Early Saturday morning she was told to remove them as permission had not been given to post them. This was bureaucracy at its best. Undaunted, she took them down and proceeded to knock on dormitory doors.

On Monday morning she called me and said, "Coach, I have three people to add to the roster, these are their names." I congratulated her and replied, "Have them come to practice today and fill out the paper work. I will take it from there."

I am sure the A.D. was surprised when I gave him our roster of eight, but he registered the team.

Now I had some breathing space and a chance to get my team together. Remember these new players were sight unseen so far as I was concerned, but I was enthusiastic. They arrived at practice, filled out the paperwork and we walked onto the court. One was an outstanding athlete but had never played tennis, another knew a little about the game but had not tried the sport, and the other one did not know what a tennis racket looked like, let alone know what to do with it. I knew immediately what my successful player/recruiter meant when she said she had three "people" to add to our list.

It was necessary that one of them had to play and I selected the athlete with the best potential to succeed. Here was a challenge that had to be met. I had about three weeks to teach her the game and get her ready for match-play. She worked like the proverbial "horse" and was able to take her place on the team in both singles and doubles showing great tenacity in doing so.

The other two never got to play in 2003 but they contributed greatly as part of the team, going to all of our matches and generating team spirit.

We finished that year with a six to four winning record and came in at third place at the season end Little East Conference Championships. To see all eight of them huddled together before each match, going into their "war-cry," was an inspiration as to what can be accomplished if you work together. I was very proud of them.

Following the completion of our season, the third week in October, it took about three weeks to complete all of the paper work to wrap up the year, return uniforms, secure the courts for winter and have a social get-together.

As a team, we were not as strong in 2004 having lost two of our top players to graduation, but we played proudly, held our heads high and set our sights on 2005.

Being that my contract as coach called for two part-time periods, I must now focus on the men's Spring match schedule which was due to commence the first week of April.

This meant getting down to business in early January. Practice would have to be indoors due to weather conditions, and must start in February if we were going to have a chance of putting our team together.

The two-month hiatus between the two seasons, which I called my vacation, went by so fast that I felt I had never stopped. What with the preliminary paper work and some recruiting seminars in that period, it felt like a full time commitment.

Things went well for the men as we started 2004. There were seven dedicated players on the roster and we got into some serious practice. We were joined by two additional players in February giving us nine starters for match play.

What a season we had. We were undefeated in conference matches and had a total winning match score of eleven to two. At our end of season Little East Conference Championships we came in at third place with only four points separating the top three teams.

It was a magnificent effort by the team and surely a guarantee of the continuation of the tennis program. We lost four of our players to graduation but recruited additional team members over the 2004 summer season which will enable us to prepare for our 2005 Spring venture.

As this chapter comes to a close we are working hard in practice sessions with the goal of doing the best we can do on the court in our up-coming matches, and to represent our university and ourselves at the highest degree of sportsmanship.

To be able to participate in helping to mold character, honesty, and the goals of achievement, through tennis, is indeed an experience to be enjoyed.

31
Marjorie—Part Two

In my courting days, marriage was more of a commitment than it is in many of cases today. There was no such thing as "try before you buy"—or, if there was, it was not visible. We were encouraged to have a nonsexual relationship before marriage which brought about a greater admiration and appreciation for each other. Getting to know each other's likes and dislikes, and understanding feelings and habits as individuals, created a bond that would survive without sex, if the occasion arose either by need or choice.

Intimacy was the consummation of marriage and would become part of the love and devotion tie that created a partnership for a lifetime together.

In today's world where sex seems to be part of courtship, or the getting-to-know-you process, it seems to me that relationships of this kind often lead to "flash" love affairs, or broken short term marriages leading to divorce, children left with single parents, and a lot of unhappiness. Whatever happened to the wedding vows? Are they taken too lightly today? Is marriage for some, just a sexual romance with no real understanding of what a partnership for life means?

When Marjorie and I were married there was no question that this union was for life. We understood the meaning and commitment of love, honor, obey, in sickness and in health—and still do today.

Marjorie has had to carry the burden of many of my idiosyncrasies, bad habits and the exasperation of my long working hours, some often coming up at the last minute. My chosen profession of sports marketing, management, consulting, tennis playing and teaching, often meant business meetings sometimes going into late night hours. Add to that my tournament play, and you have a nightmarish situation.

I must admit that when I was working those ninety-hour weeks, I did not pay enough attention to the effect it had on my wife and three children. I will regret it for all the days I have left on this earth that I did not give them more time when we were growing up together.

During this time of my life I never saw Marjorie flinch from her duties as a wife and mother to our three children. She was, and still is my partner, and did more than her share in the parenthood role. Our sons were born in 1961 (Perry Scott), 1963 (Grant Stuart), and 1965 (Scott Andrew). They have all grown up to be strong young men, outstanding in character, and they possess a unique bond of brotherhood. You will often see them together socially, sharing their friendship with each other and friends, exchanging ideas, and supporting one another in daily life. To my delight, each one of them became a tennis player. Marjorie has molded them well for their futures.

Have we had our differences? Of course. Every partnership does, and any healthy marriage is no exception. I have said on occasions, that if I were Marjorie, I would have divorced myself at least three or four times. Our disagreements and debates, however, usually finish up with compromise and good common sense.

I still drive her crazy today with what I do, and the

hours it takes to do it, but can I change after all these years? Probably not.

To know that she is always there when I am mentally drained, or tired, or sick, or needing some advice, is a great comfort and deserving of great rewards. Her diligence in caring for me through almost 40 years of type 1 diabetes, with proper diet and exercise, has enabled me to achieve my goals.

It has been my good fortune in my professional life to have met with royalty and peasants and everyone in between. The goals that I had set for myself as a young man, in all walks of life, have been achieved, which means in my mind, I have been a success. Not necessarily to the world, but to myself.

This could never have happened had it not been for Marjorie. She has guided me through thick and thin, and was always there for me to turn to for debate and constructive criticism. I firmly believe that behind every successful man there is a great woman, but unfortunately a lot of men have difficulty in acknowledging that fact.

Not so in my case.

Marjorie has fulfilled every role. She has been a wonderful wife, lover, mother, nurse and home physician, mentor, comptroller, advisor, critic, secretary, guidance counselor and friend. She is still all of those things.

Thank you Marjorie, I love you.

32

Halls of Fame

Worldly rewards were not part of the scene for me as I worked as a volunteer in the game of tennis. If one is to be a true volunteer, the task that is given to you becomes the commitment that one makes to help a program or an individual.

There is one reward however, that every volunteer receives for a job well done, and that is satisfaction. Perhaps this is the greatest reward that is possible to attain.

It therefore becomes an experience to be remembered, when public recognition is bestowed on someone.

I have been more than fortunate to be a recipient on three occasions and I humbly share these events with you, the reader, through the words of the media and friends.

The International Tennis Hall of Fame

Newport, Rhode Island, USA

At the conclusion of my term as president of the Eastern Tennis Association in 1983, the Board of Directors bestowed on me a lifetime membership in this most prestigious of tennis organizations. There was no fanfare, no press headlines, simply a quiet ceremony recognizing my achievements. I am most appreciative to those who saw fit to present me with this honor.

The Newtown Sports Hall of Fame

Newtown, Connecticut, USA

In August of 2001, I received a telephone call from the sports editor of the *Newtown Bee* newspaper, advising me that I was to be inducted into the Newtown Sports Hall of Fame. It was a surprise, because I felt that there were many more deserving recipients than I. However, it was a fact, and I was deeply moved to be included in a group of outstanding sports personalities from my home town. The following is the press article written by Kim J. Harmon, sports editor of the *Newtown Bee*.

> It has been said that tennis is the sport of a lifetime and Alex. Aitchison—from his years as promotion manager for Dunlop Australia Limited (1951–1966) to the time he was named Tennis Man of the Year by the Newtown Tennis Association (1998)—has certainly shown the veracity of that statement.
>
> To get any real grasp on how much Alex. has accomplished in the sport of tennis, all you have to do is page through his resume, all five pages of it. It's all there, too—the position as general manager of the Lawn Tennis Association of Victoria (1966–1972); the position as chairman and chief executive officer of the Port Washington Tennis Academy (1972–1985); his two singles championships from the Ringwood Tennis Club in Australia (1962–63 and 1963–64); and his representation of Australia, as an Aussie living in the US, in the Stevens Cup on the Men's Senior International teams competition (1980–1984).
>
> And so much more.

Yes, it's all there. Alex., who started playing in 1940, when he was nine, earning court time by doing chores at his brother's club, accomplished quite a bit before he and his wife Marjorie moved to Newtown in 1992. But his impact on tennis didn't stop—oh no, it continued on, and for everything he has done up to now Alex. Aitchison is being inducted into the Newtown Sports Hall of Fame.

As president of the Newtown Tennis Association in 1994, 1995 and 1996, he resurrected the rules and regulations and wrote an NTA constitution. Then he began to work on getting sponsors to help run the tournaments such as the Newtown Open, the Bertram Stroock Memorial, the Junior Championships, free Adult and Junior clinics, the Inter-town Junior Tennis Team, and the Laurel Cup team competition.

In 1997, Alex., who also coached the Immaculate High School in Danbury, worked as an honorary consultant to the Newtown Parks and Recreation Department in its project to renovate the Dickinson Park and Treadwell Park tennis facilities. He compiled and submitted a study paper to Parks and Rec. through the NTA.

And he continues to remain busy. Alex.—listed in the International Who's Who of Tennis—still maintains his business, Tennis Consultants International, which is a management and consulting service to clubs, associations, organizations and individuals. He also maintains affiliations with the International Tennis Hall of Fame in Newport, Rhode Island (as a lifetime member); the United States Tennis Association (as a lifetime member); Tennis Australia (official U.S. representative); The Australian Davis Cup Foundation (official U.S. representative); the International Clubs of Australia and the United States (as a member) and is still sponsored by Dunlop/Slazenger for his tennis rackets, clothing and accessories. Phew!!

But Alex.—listed as a Town Notable at the Edmond Town Hall—does have a life outside of tennis. He helps raise funds for charity, drives for the Newtown Meals on Wheels and is also a Luminaria volunteer (he gets to screw in the light bulbs for the annual Christmas tree lighting in Newtown).

He told me that he gets the most enjoyment and satisfaction out of showing youngsters how to hit a tennis ball and seeing the smile on their faces when it really happens; and to see the Meals on Wheels recipients who are waiting for their meal and that precious conversation of maybe 30 seconds. His ambition is to continue helping people as long as he can and to pass on to those he meets on the court the simple axiom of the sport. "If you like to play tennis," he said, "you can play it for the rest of your life. It's the sport for a lifetime."

Eastern Tennis Hall of Fame

Harrison, New York, USA

Perhaps the greatest of my experiences in the game was my induction into this Hall of Fame that houses so many giants of the sport who have excelled on the court, and those who have served the game unselfishly. As the general chairman of this organization in 1988 and 1989, joining these icons was indeed an honor. I am extremely humbled by this occasion in my life, which was held at the United Nations in New York, on April 19th, 2002, and I will treasure it forever.

Here are some excerpts from newspaper articles and the induction ceremony.

Kim J. Harmon, *Newtown Bee,* Connecticut, USA, Sports Editor.

Aitchison Heading to Hall

With a life already filled with many accolades, Alex. Aitchison of Newtown has now been named to the Eastern Tennis Hall of Fame. His induction into the Eastern Tennis Hall of Fame honors him for service to tennis in the United States (in particular the Eastern section) over the past 30 years.—His induction will have him joining such legends as Arthur Ashe, Don Budge, Vitas Gerulaitis, Althea Gibson, John McEnroe and William "Bill" Talbert. Alex.'s work has brought him in contact with world class players from all over the globe and he has served on just about every committee for the United States Tennis Association—including the Olympics, Junior Davis Cup, the National Junior Tennis Council and the National Executive Board. He has also been a guest speaker at International and National Tennis Teachers Conferences.

The News-Times, Danbury, Connecticut, USA. Chip Reid, Journalist:

Tennis Pro Being Honored as Super Volunteer

In a time when athletes worry more about endorsements than wins, when money, not passion, is the main reason for playing, Alex. Aitchison is a throwback.

An Australian, he has been instrumental in fostering the development of America's junior tennis programs, primarily as a coach and consultant. While he came to the United States in 1972 to run what was then the most prestigious junior program in the country, Aitchison has remained active in the sport and spent many long hours as a volunteer for the love of the game. His dedication has earned him induction into the Eastern Tennis Hall of Fame.

Though he may downplay his accomplishments, the

modern generation of American professional tennis players owes a great deal to the Australian. He has worked with some of the best American tennis players when they were youngsters, including John McEnroe and Tracy Austin. Aitchison, however, refuses to take credit when a player he has mentored reaches the pro circuit. 'Nobody ever makes a great player,' he told me. 'Anybody who takes credit for doing that is wrong. It's up to the player to put in the work and have the determination to be a professional.'

Eastern Tennis Hall of Fame

Hall of Fame Journal, United Nations, New York USA. Nancy Gill McShea, Editor:

If you were involved in junior tennis in any capacity during the 1970s and 1980s, and especially if you spent any time at the Port Washington Tennis Academy on Long Island, you remember that everybody was jockeying for position to curry favor with Alex. Aitchison.

During that time, which coincided with the tennis boom in New York, Aitchison was one of a handful of the game's administrators who elevated the status of junior tennis in this country and around the world. He was the chairman and chief executive officer of the Port Academy, and in 1977 he founded and directed the famous Rolex International Junior Championships there. At the same time, he was an influential officer of the Eastern Tennis Association, serving as the section's president in 1982 and '83, and before that, as vice president. He was also the chairman of both the ETA and U.S.T.A. Junior Councils and was the first person to be commissioned to formulate plans for a national junior development program and training center.

He was the right person for the job. Not only did he fit the poster image of a proper tennis official, looking crisp and dignified in his navy blazer while doing Rolex TV commentary alongside John Barrett, the BBC's voice of Wimbledon, but he also had that unhurried manner any executive strives for, particularly one who's directing a frenetic junior tennis tournament.

Aitchison's frame of reference growing up in his native Australia prepared him for the role. When he began playing tennis in the early 1940s, "there were tennis courts on every corner just like there are gas stations here," he said. With a twinkle in his eye he admits, "I moved into sports promotion when it was decided that I was not going to do anything brilliant on the court." In 1971, when he was the chief administrator of the Lawn Tennis Association of Victoria, which conducted the Australian Open, his friend, the great Australian Davis Cup Coach, Harry Hopman, called and asked him to join him in the United States.

Aitchison, at age 41, and his wife Marjorie arrived in the U.S. with their three children—Perry, Grant and Scott—and the whole family soon became involved in American tennis. Alex and the boys were all ranked Eastern players and Marjorie worked side by side with her husband at every tournament he directed. They had such a high profile, that in 1987 the Aitchison family was honored as Eastern's "Tennis Family of the Year" and in 1992 Alex. received the "Tennis Man of the Year" award.

"Alex. is handsome, charming, and with his Australian accent, he could have been the pied piper of women's league tennis," says his friend Doris Herrick, who worked closely with Aitchison during her tenure as Eastern's executive director. "Instead, he was the consummate administrator of our junior effort, setting us up to rank as one of the elite junior programs in the country.

He was also a member of more than 13 U.S.T.A. national committees and the administrator, tournament director and/or chairman of a host of adult and junior competitive events, including several U.S.T.A. Satellite Circuits: Lionel, Avon and American Express, among them

(1972–'78); the 21-and-under World Amateur Championships (the Chiquita Cup); the Girls' 12, 14 and 16 National Indoor Championships; the U.S. Olympic National Sports Festival; the Olympic Tennis Qualifying Trials; and the U.S. Open qualifying rounds.

He worked with Ivan Lendl and Martine Navratilova when he was president of the tennis division of S.T.A.R.T.—an acronym for sports technique and reaction training—when both players were No. 1 in the world.

But junior tennis was his legacy. At the helm of the Rolex Championships from 1977 to 1986 at Port Washington, it became the most famous and largest junior tennis tournament in the world, so it was no surprise when U.S.T.A. President Randy Gregson appointed Aitchison in May of 1985 as the personal consultant to the president and a special committee, to establish a player development program in the United States.

Together, they mapped out a plan, wrote a basic formal program and submitted it to the U.S.T.A. Board, which approved it. The original idea was to have a national facility in a climate that was conducive to all-year-round play with regional programs feeding into it.

"The system works," Aitchison explains, "We now have a wonderful facility in Florida and another in California serving the best players in the nation and I feel very proud in the part that I played in getting it off the ground."

He was also the first general chairman of this Hall of Fame and pioneered the criteria of recognizing those people who have performed a service to the game in the East.

Now it's your year, Alex. Congratulations!

The Presentation

My presenter was my good friend Barbara Williams, herself an inductee in 1990, and these are her words:

In 1972, Alex. Aitchison, his wife Marj, and their family, arrived from Australia to begin his work at the Port Washington Tennis Academy as general manager. Eventually he would become Director of Programs and Chief Executive Officer.

I was indeed fortunate to have met our honoree soon after he arrived in this country.

Not long after his arrival, the number of students at Port Washington grew to over 1200 students and a staff of 20 teaching professionals. Alex. began an innovative junior program designed to not only enhance the skill level, but to encourage the student to strive for the highest ideals of sportsmanship and character.

Hundreds of tournaments were held at Port in every age group for juniors and adults, and every player was required to adhere to the highest standards of sportsmanship that he had set. He began the first prize money tournament for senior women and championed that cause. He was the founder of the Rolex International Junior Championships, which became the premier junior tournament for world class junior players.

Alex. was one of the first tournament directors to see that sponsorship of tennis had an immense future and pursued this field with great diligence. He was and is a natural fund raiser for many charities including The Junior Tennis Foundation.

He served for 8 years on the Maureen Connelly Brinker International Girls' Team Championships Committee, the United States versus Australia landmark competition, and he was chairman of this Eastern Tennis Hall of Fame in 1988 and 1989.

A graduate of Melbourne University, Melbourne, Australia, with an associate degree in business administration, he was employed by the Dunlop Sports Company as its Sports Promotion Manager. Later he went to the Lawn Tennis Association of Victoria in Melbourne, Australia, as its

General Manager and Chief Executive Officer, where among other duties, he was responsible for the conduct of, the Australian Open Championships, the Davis Cup, and other special events. He worked closely with the legendary Harry Hopman in the training of Australian Davis Cup players and leading Australian juniors.

Alex. has had a fine playing career, achieving many tournament titles in Australia and being ranked in several age categories in U.S.T.A. events.

I remember one year, he was winning our Eastern Hard-Courts. It was an extremely windy day and his opponent was having a difficult time. As they crossed at the net on a change-over, Alex. gave his opponent some advice on how to overcome the problem. You guessed it, his advice was so good, he lost the match.

Tennis was always a family affair for Alex., Marj, Perry, Grant and Scott. All three boys were outstanding players and highly ranked in the Eastern Tennis Association and the United States Tennis Association. Marj and Alex. were a forceful mixed doubles team, mainly because Marj was so outstanding in the back court when Alex. would attempt to poach.

The ETA has been so fortunate in having Alex. as a volunteer for 30 years. He was the Association president in 1982 and 1983 and currently serves on the ETA Board of Directors. The family was selected the ETA Family of the year in 1987 and Alex. was the Tennis Man of the Year in 1992. He has continued his service to tennis in his new community of Newtown, Connecticut as president of the Newtown Tennis Association, where he was named their Tennis Man of the Year in 1998. He was inducted into the Newtown Sports Hall of Fame in 2001.

I would be remiss if I did not tell you of his outstanding contribution at the national level. While he was chairman of the U.S.T.A. National Junior Tennis Council, U.S.T.A. President Randy Gregson commissioned Alex. to establish the criteria and teaching methods for a national player development program, and to set in motion the establishment of a group of training centers throughout the United States. This program is now in effect and is ongoing.

Innovation is a hallmark with Alex. as is his caring and attention to his family and everyone he makes contact with.

Alex., congratulations. I am privileged to have you as my friend.

My Acceptance Speech

The master of ceremonies, Harry Marmion, had allocated three minutes for my response and great sighs went up when I took my notes from my pocket, as they measured all the way to the floor. Of course this was a ploy, and I was able to keep my remarks to about ten minutes. Here were my comments:

"Ladies and gentlemen, first, let me thank the nomination and selection committees for considering me and bestowing on me this great honor. I am extremely humbled to be joining such illustrious inductees that have come before me. Secondly, thank you, Barbara, for being my presenter. You probably know me better than anyone else in tennis and I, too, am privileged to be your friend. Your words will be cherished always. To my friends who have traveled from far distances to be here tonight, and to all of you who are friends not only to me, but to the game of tennis, thank you for your support of this great cause. Of course, there are a few who do not like me, but that goes with the territory.

I have been fortunate over the years to have worked and played with all levels of players, from beginners to world champions, and have been able to discuss our sport with administrators, press, politicians, mayors, governors and even royalty.

I started my volunteer career at 16 years of age with a local church club in Melbourne, Australia, and 56 years later, I am still enjoying serving the great game of tennis.

I have so many memories, I don't know where to start. (This is where I pulled out my 60 inches of notes.)

On May 25th of 1972, my wife Marjorie and I arrived from Australia with our three sons, Perry, Grant and Scott. We docked at New York harbor from one of the last big passenger liners to visit New York. We were met by my friend Harry Hopman, Australia's legendary Davis Cup captain, who had come to the United States a year earlier. We were transported to the Port Washington Tennis Academy, where I was to take up the task as general manager. On arrival we were introduced to the owner and staff, given lunch and before I knew it, I was seated at the tournament desk where I helped for a while, to run my first tournament for the ETA. It was the Memorial Day Championships.

In the succeeding 30 years, I have worked in almost every aspect of the game and I cannot begin to express the pleasure that comes from being part of a dedicated group, such as the East is blessed with.

During the early years, it was my great pleasure to meet and have two junior players at Port and those two are also part of this ceremony tonight. They are of course, Kathleen Horvath and Paul Annacone. One of the great rewards of working with juniors is to see them mature through the various stages of success. These two players have done this on the world scene. They have graduated with honors, and carved their own niche in history.

Another of our inductees tonight is Bob Ryland. Bob has always and still is, doing his thing quietly in the background. He is forever providing opportunities to all those who seek him out. He is a role model for every player and teacher.

I am extremely privileged to be part of this group tonight.

However, none of what I have achieved in my tennis life would have been possible if it had not been for my wife Marjorie. I have often said that behind every successful man, there is a more successful woman, and this has been so in my case. Marjorie has for 43 years been my partner on the court, my companion, my critic, my policy setter, my friend, my guidance counselor, a great wife in sickness and in health, and a fabulous mother to our three wonderful sons.

To Perry, Grant and Scott, thanks for making the family process work. Thanks for being there with your mother while I was doing my thing. You are fine gentlemen, you are extremely talented both on and off the court. I am proud to have you as my sons.

I would like to close with these few words.

If by chance, since I came
My work has brought me tennis fame
I humbly accept the accolades
Remembering the important thing
Is really the game

        Thank you all.

33

Treasures

I suppose most people have treasures that they have accumulated during their lifetime and I am sure that each one has a significant meaning. Some of course are reserved for the rich and famous and comprise artifacts, jewelry and collectibles that are often priceless. The question comes to mind, "Are these real treasures? Or, do they only represent the wealth that was available to procure them?"

My treasures are certainly not in this category, they are simply reminders of relationships that have had a meaning for me during my lifetime.

When I think back and wonder why I kept them in the first place, my memory will focus in on what these treasures are all about, and that is what makes them valuable to me.

My wife has often likened me to a squirrel, busily hoarding away the "feast" that will be consumed at some other time, and I do not entirely disagree with her. I have been known to "squirrel away" things that are not treasures. A tour of my workshop will reveal a variety of wood pieces in all sizes and shapes, bits of wire, plastic lids, enough string and rope to tie up a boat (which I do not have), old ceiling fan blades, empty tennis ball cans by the hundreds (I swear I will find some valuable thing to do with them one day), and all sorts of paraphernalia that eventually "may" be of use.

There were never any family heirlooms, but my mother did pass on to me a pure white silk scarf and a precious gem that belonged to my father. I have no memories of him as he passed away when I was two years of age. Somehow my mother had preserved that part of him for all those years and provided me with these tangible bonds that eluded me in my youth.

Family photographs take a prominent place in the treasure chest and bring back memories of days gone by. It is always a thoughtful time and one that holds your attention, irrespective of how many repeat sessions we have.

My sister Jean and brother-in-law John and his wife Margaret are invaluable when we reminisce, and provide great pleasure when we communicate across the waters separating Australia and the United States.

I am not likely to become a Mason, but I value the holding of my grandfather's, on my mother's side, Masonic Lodge Grand Masters Medallion, passed on to me after my mother's death.

A fob pocket compass hangs on our wall that belonged to my grandfather, on my father's side. Made of polished copper, it still functions accurately to this day.

Players and coaches representing their nations have bestowed on me numerous plaques, flags, medals, certificates and gifts as a token of friendship between their lands and ours. I can never express the degree of unity that existed as these exchanges took place.

More than my fair share of trophies and awards came my way for various contributions to the game, both as a participant and a volunteer. I am extremely humble that I was victorious on the court on a few occasions and that I was able to serve the game as a volunteer for nearly six decades.

The pleasure of raising money for various charities using tennis as the vehicle is a great treasure. Knowing that someone, somewhere, was helped by the effort, is the driving force that creates the motivation to do more.

Of all of the treasures, the ones to be most cherished are the memories. While the tangibles may disappear over time, the memories will fill the chest to overflowing and remain with me through sanity. Fond memories bring you together with the happenings and result in great pleasure. I am sure I could fill a book with them.

Being a player, coach and administrator in tennis for most of my life has provided me with enough reflections from this exciting and wonderful sport, to last me forever.

When a friend asked me recently how long I had been playing the game, and I explained, "A mere sixty-six years," it triggered the memory of how it all started for me.

Sweeping the courts, sneaking a few hits with my brother, school tennis, climbing the rungs of the "level ladder," competition, working in the sport, administration of the game and achieving the goals that I had set for myself.

If I never have another book to write or read, I will just dig into my treasure chest, bring out my memories, settle down for the rest of my life, and enjoy the experience.

34
Closure

The last chapter of any book is the most difficult to write, particularly if one is still active in life and tennis as I am.

Trying to decide where to finish this series of experiences was extremely frustrating as my tennis involvement just seems to go on and on. It appears that anything beyond this closure will have to be in another book at another time.

In the meantime, keep playing this great game of tennis, until you drop.

About the Author

Alex. Aitchison was born in Melbourne, Australia, in 1931. His involvement in tennis commenced at the early age of eight when he frequented the public courts where his brother George was a teaching professional. There he started to climb the rungs of the tennis ladder and eventually over a span of more than six decades, participated in every facet of the game.

This book is a unique masterpiece in that it shows the diversity of the man who wrote it.
Not an international star player (although he played senior international competition), but one who has shared the glory with many of the world's best, by being involved as their tournament director, administrator or mentor.
Conducting Davis Cup competition, International Championships, national events, assisting in Federation Cup play and all levels below, right down to helping a child hit his/her first tennis ball, was, and still is, his forte.
His administrative career started in Australia where he was the Chief Executive Officer of the Lawn Tennis Association of Victoria with some three hundred thousand registered players, and General Manager of the internal club, and its four thousand individual members. He was responsible for the conduct of the Australian Open, State Championships and numerous other major events.
Some of his activities before his introduction into big

time administration are described in his writings, where he took on tasks that on some occasions, could have led to his death, but as he said, they provided the money necessary for him to be involved in our great game.

It was the good fortune of the United States Tennis Association that he came to this country in 1972, taking on the role of Chief Executive Officer and General Manager of the Port Washington Tennis Academy in New York. Here he worked with the legendary Harry Hopman, administering the training of junior hopefuls, as he had done with him in Australia.

High profile names like Mary Carillo, Peter Fleming, Vitas Gerulaitis and John McEnroe, to name a few, were in junior programs at "Port," and Tracy Austin and Bjorn Borg practiced there frequently, as did many of the players coming in to play the U.S. Open.

He soon became involved with the Eastern Tennis Association, serving as its president in 1982–83, and also with the United States Tennis Association where he was a member of numerous national committees including, Junior Davis Cup, Junior Tennis Council (serving as chairman in 1985–86), Olympics, U.S. Open Junior Championships and U.S. Open qualifying rounds. He also served as a personal consultant to U.S.T.A. President Randy Gregson, and a special committee in 1985, to set up a national player development program, which is in place today.

The chapters take us through some of his experiences from early childhood and cover over six decades of tennis participation as seen through his eyes.

It is refreshing to have a tennis book published that does not linger on instruction alone, but rather gives us a perspective of what is behind the role the writer played in various events.

The spectrum of the story covers a wide array of circumstances and tells us of the vast number of people who have been fortunate enough to meet and benefit from the author's expertise.

He truly is a legend in our game, having excelled as an administrator, author, consultant, guest speaker, player, tournament director, teacher and TV/Radio host and commentator.

203 270-8218